Strengthening Credibility

A LEADER'S WORKBOOK

JAMES M. KOUZES AND BARRY Z. POSNER
WITH JANE BOZARTH

JOSSEY-BASS
A Wiley Imprint
www.josseybass.com

CONTENTS

Preface   *v*

1 Leadership Is a Relationship   1

2 Credibility Makes a Difference   19

3 Discipline 1: Discover Yourself   33

4 Discipline 2: Appreciate Constituents   59

5 Discipline 3: Affirm Shared Values   79

6 Discipline 4: Develop Capacity   97

7 Discipline 5: Serving a Purpose   115

8 Discipline 6: Sustain Hope   135

9 The Struggle to Be Human   165

Characteristics of an Admired Leader   177

About the Authors   *179*

PREFACE

Our book *Credibility: How Leaders Gain and Lose It, Why People Demand It* is about what constituents look for and admire in leaders and the implications of those expectations for aspiring and practicing leaders. It is also about how leaders earn the trust and confidence of their constituents. It's about what people demand of their leaders as a prerequisite to willingly contributing their hearts, minds, bodies, and souls. It's about the actions leaders must take in order to intensify their constituents' commitment to a common cause.

Through extensive research, we found that credibility is not based on job titles or hierarchical positions but with the human being in the leader's shoes. Above all else, we found that *leadership is personal*. It's not about the corporation, the community, or the country. It's about *you* and your *relationship* with others. If people don't believe in the *messenger*, they won't believe the message. If people don't believe in *you*, they won't believe in what *you* say. And if it's about you, then it's about your beliefs, your values, and your principles. It's also about how true you are to your values and beliefs.

This workbook is meant to help you take a credibility journey of your own. You will be asked to reflect on your beliefs and values, examine your actions as they impact the perception of you as a messenger, and explore ways to nurture your relationship with and the commitment of those you serve.

Who This Workbook Is for

This workbook is designed for anyone who wishes to have significant influence and strengthen his or her credibility. While much of the workbook references people in specific organizational roles (private- and public-sector), it is also appropriate for those involved in school, volunteer, family, or community activities.

What This Workbook Will Do for You

Leadership is a journey, not a destination. It's important for leaders to take time for continual development and to make time for intentional reflection. This workbook is meant to help you think through the current state—where you are now in terms of your abilities and relationships with constituents—while asking you to also articulate the desired future state for yourself, those around you, and your organization.

How This Workbook Is Organized

This workbook is meant to accompany *Credibility: How Leaders Gain and Lose It, Why People Demand It*. While it is designed to work as a standalone—with content from the book briefly encapsulated—you will benefit most from reading *Credibility* and using this workbook as a companion, working through the activities in each chapter after having read the book. The workbook is organized as a partner for the book and is arranged to match *Credibility's* nine chapters. In most cases the subheadings in the workbook match those of the main text. We recommend that you work through the chapters in order, as in some cases information in one chapter is built on information set forth in an earlier one.

Completing the Activities

This workbook invites you to engage in a good amount of self-reflection; the more honest you are with yourself, the better. Take your time with the activities. Some ask for you to recall a past incident and reexamine it. Others ask you to take an honest assessment of yourself now. Investing time and thought into these activities will make them more useful for you and will help move you toward your goal of becoming a more credible leader. Try to answer honestly, and try to execute the action plans you create. Calendaring will help with this, as will sharing your insights and plans with others.

A credible leader understands that he or she is not an island: the leader's success depends on the cooperation and support of those being led. A number of activities in this workbook are designed for use with the work team, clients, or others on whom the leader depends. Instructions are given for carrying these out, but are meant to be flexible according to the setting, the people involved, and their locations. Adapt them to make them work for you.

The quest to become a better leader is never easy, it is always full of challenges, but when everything comes together, it brings out the best in you and in others. We wish you the best in this endeavor.

Jim Kouzes
Barry Posner
Spring 2011

CHAPTER ONE

Leadership
Is a Relationship

This *Credibility* chapter explores the expectations people have of their leaders. It looks at what they look for and admire in leaders and what these preferences mean for the work of a leader. It is intended to help you gain a better understanding of the expectations people have of their leaders and what these expectations mean. Chapters 3 through 8 address each of the essentials that enact these expectations. As you complete this workbook chapter, consider these questions:

- What forms the foundation of a constructive and positive relationship between you and your constituents?
- What can you do to build and sustain that kind of relationship?

As we begin our discussion of the relationship between leaders and their constituents, reflect for a moment on the kind of leader you would most *willingly* follow. Think about the kind of leader you would voluntarily sign up to work with if given a choice. What words immediately come to mind when describing this person? Record them below:

- _____
- _____
- _____
- _____
- _____

Characteristics of Admired Leaders

For over three decades we've been asking people to answer the question: "What personal values, traits, and characteristics do you look for and admire in a leader, someone whose direction you would *willingly* follow?" How would you respond? What qualities would you put on the list?

It turns out that people look for many special qualities in their leaders. The research indicates that the attributes listed on the next page—Characteristics of Admired Leaders—account for most of these qualities. From this list of twenty attributes, please select the seven you most look for in a leader—someone whose direction you would willingly follow. Just place a check mark (✓) by seven items; there is no need to order or rank them.

Characteristics of Admired Leaders

☐ Ambitious (aspiring, hardworking, striving)

☐ Broad-Minded (open-minded, flexible, receptive, tolerant)

☐ Caring (appreciative, compassionate, concerned, loving, nurturing)

☐ Competent (capable, proficient, effective, gets the job done, professional)

☐ Cooperative (collaborative, team player, responsive)

☐ Courageous (bold, daring, risk-taker, gutsy)

☐ Dependable (reliable, conscientious, responsible)

☐ Determined (dedicated, resolute, persistent, purposeful)

☐ Fair-Minded (just, unprejudiced, objective, forgiving)

☐ Forward-Looking (visionary, foresighted, future-oriented, has direction)

☐ Honest (truthful, has integrity, trustworthy, has character, is trusting)

☐ Imaginative (creative, innovative, curious)

☐ Independent (self-reliant, self-sufficient, self-confident)

☐ Inspiring (uplifting, enthusiastic, energetic, optimistic, positive)

☐ Intelligent (bright, smart, thoughtful, intellectual, reflective, logical)

☐ Loyal (faithful, dutiful, unswerving in allegiance, devoted)

☐ Mature (experienced, wise, has depth)

☐ Self-Controlled (restrained, self-disciplined)

☐ Straightforward (direct, candid, forthright)

☐ Supportive (helpful, offers assistance, comforting)

Now think about the Characteristics of an Admired Leader from the point of view of your constituents. There is another Characteristics of an Admired Leader worksheet at the end of this workbook. Make copies of the form and pass them out to several of your constituents. Ask them to complete the worksheet and give it back to you. After gathering and looking over the worksheets, spend some time reflecting on the following questions.

How closely aligned are your own behavior and character to the seven characteristics that you chose?

_____

_____

_____

_____

_____

_____

_____

Articulate your understanding and underlying core beliefs related to your choices.

_____

_____

_____

_____

_____

How clear are you about your constituents' expectations of you? How similar are your expectations to those of your constituents?

_____

_____

_____

_____

_____

_____

_____

As you can see from the table on the next page, which displays the results of our research on the Characteristics of Admired Leaders, four characteristics—honest, forward-looking, inspiring, and competent—stand out. These four are the only four that have consistently been selected by the majority of respondents over the last three decades.

Characteristics of Admired Leaders
(Percentage of People Selecting Characteristic Over the Years)

Characteristic	2010	2002	1987
Honest	85	88	83
Forward-Looking	70	71	62
Inspiring	69	65	58
Competent	64	66	67
Intelligent	42	47	43
Broad-Minded	40	40	37
Dependable	37	33	32
Supportive	36	35	32
Fair-minded	35	42	40
Straightforward	31	34	34
Determined	28	23	20
Cooperative	26	28	25
Ambitious	26	17	21
Courageous	21	20	27
Caring	20	20	26
Imaginative	18	23	34
Loyal	18	14	11
Mature	16	21	23
Self-Controlled	11	8	13
Independent	6	6	10

Credibility Is the Foundation

The characteristics of trustworthiness, expertise, and dynamism comprise what communications researchers refer to as "source credibility."[1] In assessing the believability of sources of information—whether the president of the organization, the president of the country, a salesperson, a TV newscaster, or a product spokesperson—those who rate highly on these three characteristics are considered to be credible, believable sources of information.

These three dimensions of source credibility are synonymous with three of the top four most frequently selected qualities in the Characteristics of Admired Leaders Checklist: honest, competent, and inspiring. For trustworthiness, you can say *honest*. For expertise, you can say *competent*. For dynamism, you can say *inspiring*. In other words, what we found quite unexpectedly in our initial research, and what has been reaffirmed since, is that, above all else, people want leaders who are credible. The most important lesson we have learned from our research on what people most expect from their leaders is this: *credibility is the foundation of leadership.*

Let's explore each characteristic of admired leaders in more depth.

Honest

In our research, "honesty" is selected more often than any other characteristic as absolutely essential to leadership. What does being honest mean to you? How do you know when a leader is honest? For example, here's a situation faced in a recent staff meeting:

Leaders in a government organization, which holds "transparency" as a core value, engaged in a heated discussion. Recent bad budget news pointed to an almost inevitable likelihood of layoffs. Patricia said, "Well, I feel we are obligated to tell staff this is coming and keep them informed of news as it evolves." Chris vehemently disagreed, stating, "That will only lead to trouble and will be terrible for morale. There's no need to say anything until we know for sure who will be affected and when."

What does an "honest" leader do in this situation? What's your position on this? What would you do if you had the knowledge about future layoffs?

_____

_____

_____

_____

_____

What would be the result for you, the organization, and your constituents if you took this action? How would your decision affect relationships in the future?

_____

_____

_____

_____

_____

"Honesty" is not just telling the truth, but behaving in honest ways. Fudging expense reports, padding estimates, overpromising on services, and not saying anything at all are other ways of not being honest. So is breaking promises. Are people in your organization rewarded or punished for behaving honestly?

_____

_____

_____

_____

_____

_____

_____

As we will explore later in this workbook, trust is a critical component of credibility. It is not possible to build trust in an environment that rewards dishonesty or punishes telling the truth.

Forward-Looking

Constituents expect a leader to have a well-defined orientation toward the future. They want to know what the organization will look like, feel like, and be like when it arrives at its goal. They want you to be able to answer the question: Where are we going?

How clear are you as to where you are taking your organization? How clear are those you lead about the future you envision? Describe your view of the future of your organization, your work unit, your constituents—and yourself. How will the workplace look? What will people be doing (or not doing)? What will people have accomplished? What problems will have been solved? Where will energy be going? What will YOU be doing? Jot down some notes that you can use to later develop a more detailed picture of a shared vision for your organization.

_____

_____

_____

_____

_____

_____

_____

_____

_____

_____

_____

_____

Inspiring

People admire and respect leaders who are dynamic, uplifting, enthusiastic, positive, and optimistic. As the old maxim goes, "Enthusiasm is infectious," and people want a leader who spreads that kind of emotion for the vision and work of the organization.

Begin with yourself. What are you passionate about? How do you convey your enthusiasm and energy? In the past, how have your attempts at "inspiring" been received? What can you do to better project your dynamism and enthusiasm?

_____

_____

_____

_____

Connect with others. While people are often initially motivated when they hear passionate appeals from charismatic leaders, that early excitement wears off. How can you use your enthusiasm in continuing to inspire others? What can you do to maintain that feeling of inspiration in your followers?

_____

_____

_____

_____

Keep your energy up. What are you doing to stay energized? How are you maintaining your own sense of joy and enthusiasm at work, at home, and in the community? What are you doing to have a positive outlook on things?

_____

_____

_____

_____

Competent

If people are going to follow you, they have to believe that you know what you are doing. They must see you as having expertise in the business, in your functional area, and in leadership. The specific knowledge, skills, and abilities vary depending on your role, type of organization, and industry, but your constituents have to have confidence in your competence. Competent *leaders* are not just capable *managers* or competent *contributors*. Not only do you have to exhibit competence in your field, but you have to exhibit the leadership practices described in our book *The Leadership Challenge*: the ability to Model the Way, Inspire a Shared Vision, Challenge the Process, Enable Others to Act, and Encourage the Heart. See *The Leadership Challenge* for more detail, and the *Leadership Practices Inventory* assessment for in-depth work in each of these areas.[2]

When have you seen a leader who was inspiring, honest, and forward-looking, but who just wasn't very competent? What was your relationship with that person? How did the lack of competence affect this person's credibility?

_____

_____

_____

_____

In what areas would you say you have a high level of competence? What are your strengths? What are those areas of expertise that you and your constituents can rely on right now? Technical competence in your functional area? Taking initiative? Being a positive role model for others? Make a list of the three areas of competence in which you feel most confident.

1. _____

_____

2. _____

_____

_____

3. _____

_____

In what general areas do you feel you need to become more competent? Sticking with decisions? Communicating an inspiring vision of the future? Dealing with conflict? Encouraging others when they do a good job? Presenting ideas in public? This workbook will give you an opportunity to create and develop an improvement plan for yourself. Make a list of three areas in which you feel you need to improve your knowledge, skills, and abilities:

1. _____

_____

_____

2. _____

_____

_____

3. _____

_____

_____

Consistent Over Time

The most admired leader qualities of honest, forward-looking, inspiring, and competent have remained constant over three decades of our research. People are looking for these characteristics as much today as they ever have. Therefore, it's important that you be consistent over time in your commitment to exhibiting the behaviors that earn and sustain personal credibility. It is easy to preach "ethics" but watch the line slip when sales drop; it is easy to become excited about a new initiative but lose enthusiasm when the initial glow wears off. A leader must be consistent in actions and behavior for the long haul. Think back over the past work year. What behaviors have you espoused? What projects have you excitedly launched? What has happened since then? Have you held the line you established? Have you made too many exceptions or lost interest? What has been the result on your credibility?

_____

_____

_____

_____

_____

_____

Understanding Global and Local Expectations

Context matters. While the four most admired qualities have been consistent over time, our _credibility_ research shows, for instance, that other managers value a leader who is forward-looking more than non-managers value the quality. In some companies, "supportive" emerges as a most admired characteristic; in others, it was "courage." Workers in a medical environment would likely value "caring," whereas those in research and development might choose "imaginative."

What is your context? Do you deal mostly with managers or with non-managers? Other than the top four attributes, what other qualities are important to your work area or professional field?

_____

_____

_____

_____

_____

_____

What are the global expectations of your business, and how to they interface with the local expectations of your constituents?

_____

_____

_____

_____

_____

_____

What Is the Current Status of Your Credibility Bank Account?

Credibility is earned. It is built over time, through a history of working alongside and interacting with a leader. So far, what have you "banked" in each critical area? Rate the amount in each account on a scale from 1 (low; I need to do more in this area) to 5 (high; I have banked a lot in this account).

Characteristic	Low				High
Honest	1	2	3	4	5
Forward-Looking	1	2	3	4	5
Inspiring	1	2	3	4	5
Competent	1	2	3	4	5
Consistency Over Time	1	2	3	4	5
Understanding Global and Local Expectations	1	2	3	4	5

Now review your scores for each item. Where did you rate yourself highest? Where did you rate yourself lowest? If you rated yourself lower that a 4 on any of these assets in your credibility account, you need to ask yourself why and how you can invest in increasing those assets. Low to moderate ratings on any of these areas will decrease your overall credibility and requires attention.

Earning Credibility

The rest of this workbook will help you explore ways to fill up your bank accounts, to help establish yourself as a more credible leader. Remember: this is a journey, not a destination. There will always be room for growth and new learning. And what matters most is not doing something in the short term, but in displaying behaviors consistently. Credibility is built brick by brick over time.

Notes

1. See, for example, the classic work of D. K. Berlo, J. B. Lemert, & R. J. Mertz, "Dimensions for Evaluating the Acceptability of Message Sources," *Public Opinion Quarterly*, 1969, *33,* 563–576.

2. Kouzes, J. M., & Posner, B. Z. (2008). *The Leadership Challenge* (4th ed.). San Francisco: Jossey-Bass and Kouzes, J. M., & Posner, B. Z. (2003). *The Leadership Practices Inventory (LPI)*. San Francisco: Pfeiffer. For ordering information see www.leadershipchallenge.com/. Also see Kouzes, J. M., & Posner, B. Z. (2011). *Credibility: How Leaders Gain and Lose It, Why People Demand It*. San Francisco: Jossey-Bass.

CHAPTER TWO

Credibility Makes a Difference

Take a moment to think of a time when you willingly followed the direction of someone you admired and respected as a leader. Make some mental or written notes as you answer the following questions:

What was the situation—the project, program, or activity—in which you were involved with this person? What was the project or activity expected to accomplish?

_____

_____

_____

_____

_____

_____

What three or four words would you use to describe how you felt when you were involved with this person? How did this leader make you feel about yourself?

_____

_____

_____

What leadership actions did this person take to get you and others to want to perform at your best? What were the leadership behaviors of this person that you admired?

_____

_____

_____

_____

_____

In one sentence, summarize the impact this person had on you.

_____

_____

Credible Leaders Inspire Loyalty and Commitment

Credible leaders have a positive influence on people and organizations, while leaders who are not credible have a negative impact on morale and performance. In strengthening your credibility, it's vital to understand that *constituents will become willingly involved to the extent that they believe in those sponsoring the change.* Have you ever known a leader who was full of ideas but short on execution? Worse, have you ever been pulled into a project or initiative with little confidence that the leader could see it through? It's discouraging, and it destroys whatever credibility the leader did have. In working with your constituents, the question is not just, "Do they believe in this change?" but "Do they believe in my ability to lead it?"

Think of a time someone in authority led in a way you felt was harmful or disrespectful. Perhaps it was a teacher who ridiculed you or a supervisor who yelled at you. How did you feel in the moment? How did you feel going forward? How do you remember that person now? While you may have been obedient to that person, were you really *committed* to him or her and what you were being asked to do?

Credible leaders raise self-esteem. In the cases we collected, respondents told us time and again that credible leaders made them feel valued, motivated, and enthusiastic. They felt both challenged and capable of meeting challenges and supported as they enacted their tasks. The people you lead are the ones who will help you achieve the goals you set. Leadership isn't all about *you*. It's about *them* and the way you make them feel.

In our research the ten words most frequently used to describe admired leaders were valued, motivated, enthusiastic, challenged, inspired, capable, supported, powerful, respected, and proud.[1] Which would people say apply to your leadership?

_____

_____

_____

_____

Which are most important to you?

_____

_____

_____

_____

Which do you believe you most need to work on?

_____

_____

_____

_____

Ask yourself: What kind of a leader am I? Am I a leader who would be on someone's most admired leader list? Or am I on some other kind of list? How am I doing at helping others achieve possibilities they didn't even think possible? How am I doing at bringing out the best in others? What needs to change?

_____

_____

_____

_____

_____

_____

Credible leaders make a difference. They have a positive impact on those around them. The credibility difference is especially important in times of adversity, wrenching change, and transition. When leaders have to ask people to work harder and make sacrifices because of new challenges in the marketplace or the global economy, they need a solid foundation of credibility to build on. What are you doing to make sure your credibility is sustained not only in the good times, but also in the tough times?

Sustaining Credibility Is a Person-to-Person Activity

Whom do you trust more, the people you know or those you don't know? Trust grows from getting to know someone, from learning you can trust him or her. In the workplace, it grows out of small daily interactions, physical presence, and personal contact. People do not trust leaders they never see or who are completely inaccessible. Trust is earned by walking around, saying hello, paying attention. These don't necessarily have to be in-person communications— much can be done virtually—but it is important to pay attention to individual relationships.

What intentional actions are you taking to earn the respect and trust of your constituents? Are you visible and close to them? Are you earning credibility by physical acts like shaking hands, leaning forward, stopping to listen, being responsive, sharing your experiences, telling your story, joining in dialogue? What needs to change? How will you go about it?

_____

_____

_____

_____

_____

_____

Years ago, when still a very young man, the actor Michael J. Fox developed a cocaine problem. Years later he took responsibility for his behavior but added, "The problem with being a celebrity is that no one will ever tell you, 'No.'" That is the danger to the leader who becomes too isolated and out of touch, surrounded by only a few advisors. It may reach the point at which no one will say "No," or point out a problem, or surface some unpleasant detail, or sound a warning about a possible bad decision. It is important that leaders become known, work to get to know others, and develop relationships that have room for trust and honesty.

Credible leaders know their strengths, and they are confident enough in their abilities that they aren't afraid to hear the bad news, or an idea from a constituent who knows more than they do, or some constructive feedback about how they can improve. They are open and make themselves vulnerable by owning mistakes and asking for advice.

Rate your own willingness to be vulnerable. Imagine yourself in a group setting—a meeting or other gathering with your constituents. Rate each below on a scale of 1 to 5, with 1 being something that would be high-risk for you and 5 being something you'd be quite comfortable doing.

1. Asking for (and listening to) feedback from others.

1	2	3	4	5
High Risk				Quite Comfortable

2. Asking for help with a problem.

1	2	3	4	5
High Risk			Quite Comfortable	

3. Expressing confusion and uncertainty about a situation or decision.

1	2	3	4	5
High Risk			Quite Comfortable	

4. Admitting I was wrong.

1	2	3	4	5
High Risk			Quite Comfortable	

5. Admitting that someone has hurt my feelings.

1	2	3	4	5
High Risk			Quite Comfortable	

6. Expressing anger about a situation.

1	2	3	4	5
High Risk			Quite Comfortable	

7. Expressing gratitude to someone.

1	2	3	4	5
High Risk			Quite Comfortable	

Add your scores and check your overall willingness to be open and vulnerable with others. A score of:

28 to 35 suggests you are quite willing to be open and vulnerable

21 to 27 means you're moderately open, but have some reservations

7 to 20 suggests a low level of willingness to be open and vulnerable; you need to reflect on why this is and what you can do about it

---

A credibility check is past-oriented. It has to do with a reputation earned over time, tasks, promises, job roles, and job titles. Credibility is built day by day, stone by stone.

DWYSYWD

What is credibility *behaviorally*? How do you know it when you see it? When we asked this question in our research, people told us time and again that it was about following through on actions, being consistent in word and deed, practicing what was preached. All these phrases can be summarized in one statement: To be credible you must do what you say you will do—DWYSYWD for short.

How would you rate yourself on the DWYSYWD benchmark of personal credibility? Check the one statement below that is most true of you.

- ☐ I always do what I say I will do.
- ☐ I do my best to keep promises and commitments, but sometimes circumstances and time constraints keep me from achieving them.
- ☐ I sometimes over-promise and can't deliver what I say I will do.
- ☐ It seems I often miss doing what I say I will do; I feel I disappoint my constituents and family.

If you have trouble DWYSYWD, where do problems arise?

Do you overestimate your abilities?

Do you underestimate time requirements or resources needed?

Do you need to secure more support and backing before you begin?

Do you have a hard time saying, "No," but then have trouble delivering what you promise?

Write out ways in which you can overcome any of these challenges:

_____

_____

_____

_____

_____

_____

_____

_____

_____

In building *leadership* credibility, the "do what you say" message goes further: You and your constituents must do what WE say WE will do. You are not just leading yourself. You are leading a group of people who share a set of values and a vision. On the standard of *leadership* credibility—DWYSYWD—how do you rate yourself? (Again, select the one statement that is most true of you and your constituents.)

☐ We have a reputation for achieving targets and delivering what we promise.
☐ We usually achieve what we say we will do.
☐ We have trouble doing what we say we will do.
☐ We have a reputation for dropping the ball or failing to achieve targets.

Do you overestimate constituent abilities or fail to understand their availability and other commitments? Do you fail to enable them or provide tools so they can deliver what is promised? Are they constrained by bureaucracy or rules that inhibit performance? Write out your plan for overcoming these challenges:

_____

_____

_____

_____

_____

_____

Is what you say aligned with what constituents understand and believe? Is what you say consistent with what they want? Are you on the same path? To what extent are your aims and aspirations congruent with those of constituents— or not? What needs to change?

How would you rate yourself and your constituents on the clarity, unity, and intensity elements of leadership credibility?

- Are you *clear* about the message?
- Are you *unified* around shared intentions?
- Are you *intensely committed* to actions that are consistent with the message?

To what extent are you clear and in agreement on values and visions and putting your energies and resources behind making the promises real?

_____

_____

_____

_____

_____

_____

The Six Disciplines for Earning and Sustaining Credibility

Take a look back at the case example you wrote about at the beginning of the chapter, the one about the admired leader you willingly followed. Look specifically at the actions that person took to earn your respect and confidence— the behaviors that he or she demonstrated and the ones that you felt made the difference. Write them out again here:

_____

_____

_____

When we analyzed the lists of behaviors in the cases we collected in our research for _Credibility,_ we were able to identify six core disciplines for earning and sustaining credibility. We will look at each discipline more closely in the

29

coming workbook chapters. Briefly consider each and reflect on your current status. Do you exhibit any, some, or all of the six disciplines? To what extent would your constituents say these six disciplines accurately describe your behaviors, activities, and areas of focus?

1. Discover Your Self

Do you know, and can you articulate, who you are, what you believe in, and what you stand for?

2. Appreciate Constituents

Do you possess a deep understanding of the collective values and desires of your constituents?

3. Affirm Shared Values

Have you worked with your constituents to find common ground? Are your constituents united behind a common cause?

4. Develop Capacity

In what ways are you continually educating your constituents? How are they enabled to keep themselves informed and their skills up-to-date? Do they work in an atmosphere of continual learning?

5. Serve a Purpose

Who and what do you serve? Why this and not something else?

6. Sustain Hope

In what ways do you exhibit optimism about the future and confidence in your constituents? How are you keeping hope alive?

Reflect

Before moving on to the next chapter, take a moment to reflect on the six disciplines. Earning and sustaining credibility is hard work over the long haul. Living the six disciplines is a challenge every day, forever. Be honest with yourself: How committed are you to doing the hard work required to earn and maintain credibility over time? What do you need to do to build your own commitment?

Note

1. Kouzes, J. M., & Posner, B. Z. (2011). *Credibility: How Leaders Gain and Lose It, Why People Demand It.* San Francisco: Jossey-Bass.

CHAPTER THREE

Discipline 1: Discover Yourself

Your ability to earn and sustain credibility depends first and foremost on how well you know yourself. It depends on how well you know your values and beliefs, your skills and deficiencies, what success means to you, and the level of commitment you are willing to make. The better you know yourself, the better you can make sense of the often incomprehensible and conflicting messages you receive daily. Do this, do that. Buy this, buy that. Support this, support that. Decide this, decide that. You need internal guidance to navigate the turmoil in today's highly uncertain environment.

Your credibility journey begins with the process of self-discovery. Our research indicates that, to genuinely know the level of commitment you are willing to make, you must discover three essential aspects of yourself: your credo, your areas of competence, and your level of self-confidence.

Compose Your Personal Credo

You can't do what you say if you don't know what you believe. The first stage of your credibility journey is to clarify your values and determine the roots of your personal credo.

Where did your beliefs about what is important in life come from?

Let's revisit your childhood, say, until you were ten years old. This is when you learned to think and act and navigate in the world. Think about parents, relatives, neighbors, friends, and teachers who influenced you.

What do you remember being told about how to act and what to think? Do you remember hearing "If you can't say anything nice, don't say anything at all"? How about, "Don't be such a tomboy" or "boys don't cry"? or "You must respect your elders"? Did you hear that work could be exciting and meaningful, or drudgery to be carried out? What were your beliefs about education? What shaped your beliefs about marriage and family? What did you learn about money and the definition of success or failure? What were the implicit messages about happiness, or making mistakes, or asserting yourself? Briefly write down the messages you learned about what others expected of you:

_____

_____

_____

_____

_____

_____

_____

_____

Which of these ideas or principles still guide you now?

_____

_____

_____

_____

_____

_____

Which are still useful? How do they help, support, or guide you in your daily life now?

_____

_____

_____

_____

_____

_____

Which are no longer useful? Do any ever cause you conflict or uneasiness? Is it time to let go of some old ways of thinking and acting?

_____

_____

_____

_____

_____

_____

How can you know whether you or others truly hold a value? Here are some questions to ask yourself about each of your values.[1]

- Did I freely choose this value? If it is an organizational value, do I freely choose to accept it?
- Have I considered other alternatives to this value and explored them fully?
- Have I considered the alternative consequences of this value?
- Do I truly cherish this value? Is it something I prize? Am I passionate about it?
- Am I willing to publicly affirm that I hold this value?
- Am I willing to act on this value?
- Am I willing to act on this value repeatedly, over time, in a consistent pattern?

If your answers to all these questions are "Yes," then you are valuing your choices. If you have said "No" to any of them, then you might want to spend some time reexamining the values you have chosen.

"This I Believe"

Visit the "This I Believe" website at http://thisibelieve.org. "This I Believe" is a nonprofit organization that invites people of all ages and backgrounds to share short essays about their guiding principles and core beliefs. Essays provided in print and via audio are brief and clear; some amusing, many touching, all deeply personal. Browse themes relevant to your business life or personal interests. One favorite of leaders is an essay acknowledging the creativity of janitors and construction workers. Another favorite: the belief in being good to the pizza delivery guy. Start with the "about" tab on the website to learn more about the project, then try "explore" to browse for themes. (Many of the essays have been compiled in book form as well.)

Now try writing a "This I Believe" essay of your own. In composing it, first reflect on your past. Consider things that formed and influenced you. What books made the biggest impression on you as a child, and what values do these books espouse? Who are your most admired political leaders, and what do they believe? What older persons in your early life did you admire, and what did you learn from them? Can you recall suffering in your early life—yours or someone else's? How did you react? What did you learn from the experience? What do you feel about work and its relationship to a purposeful life?

Having reflected on your personal experience, write a brief statement of three hundred to five hundred words. Provide a context about your beliefs—it could be around your job, your community, your family—and tell a story that grounds what you believe in your life. Don't just make a long list of several beliefs, but instead write an essay about only one or two. Make sure to include a statement that begins with "I believe that . . . ." (You might want to compose this on a separate sheet of paper or on your computer.)

_____

_____

_____

_____

_____

_____

_____

_____

_____

_____

_____

_____

_____

_____

_____

_____

Let Your Values Be Your Guide

It is not enough to have values; a leader must demonstrate them. If you hold a value that does not appear on the list, simply add that word in one of the blank spaces at the end of the list. From the list below, circle the five values you hold most dear. Then, using a 1 to 5 scale (where 1 = rarely and 5 = almost always), assign a candid rating of how often you display, work toward achieving, or otherwise live each of the values you select.

Achievement/Success	Autonomy	Beauty
Challenge	Communication	Competence
Competition	Courage	Creativity
Curiosity	Decisiveness	Dependability
Discipline	Diversity	Effectiveness
Empathy	Equality	Family
Flexibility	Freedom	Friendship
Growth	Happiness	Harmony
Health	Honesty/Integrity	Hope
Humor	Independence	Innovation
Intelligence	Love/Affection	Loyalty
Open-Mindedness	Patience	Power
Productivity	Prosperity/Wealth	Quality
Recognition	Respect	Risk-Taking
Security	Service	Simplicity
Spirituality/Faith	Strength	Teamwork
Trust	Truth	Variety
Wisdom		

(The values activity above is also available in the form of a card deck. To order *The Leadership Challenge Values Cards*, visit www.leadershipchallenge .com; click on the Products link and then the Training Materials link. For more information, email leadership@wiley.com.)

Once you have identified your core values, write them in priority in the spaces below, and answer the question, "Why is this value important to me?" for each one.

Value 1: _____

Is most important to me

because _____

_____

_____

_____

_____

Value 2: _____

Is important to me

because _____

_____

_____

_____

_____

Value 3: _____

Is important to me

because _____

_____

_____

_____

_____

Value 4: _____

Is important to me

because _____

_____

_____

_____

_____

Value 5: _____

Is important to me

because _____

_____

_____

_____

_____

Finally, for each of your top five core values, ask yourself how strongly you believe in it. Which ones would you stand up for, fight, die, or go to jail for?

Further Values Clarification: What Do You Value in Others?

Imagine that you were being sent to open a new office in another part of the world. This is a huge promotion and enormous opportunity for you. You may take five of your constituents (including colleagues, customers, other leaders, etc.) with you. You have one year to make the new office a success; if at the end of that time you have failed, then all of you will lose your jobs.

Which five people would you choose to join you in opening that office?

1. _____

2. _____

3. _____

4. _____

5. _____

Why? Think not just about what skills each person has (you could, for instance, find any number of people who could competently keep the books) but what values he or she holds. Does one always keep promises while another values cooperation and negotiation? Does one consistently tell you the truth, even when it may be hard for you to hear? Does one always remain calm despite chaos around her? Why would you want each of these individuals?

_____

_____

_____

_____

_____

Credo Memo

As a way of summarizing your values into a one-page statement, write a Credo Memo to those you work with most closely. Here's the setup: Imagine that your organization has afforded you the chance to take a six-month sabbatical, all expenses paid. The only hitch is that you may not take any work along on this sabbatical. And you will not be permitted to communicate to anyone at your office or plant while you are away—not by letter, phone, fax, e-mail, or other means. Just you, a few good books, some music, and your family or a friend.

But before you depart, those with whom you work need to know the principles that you believe should guide their actions in your absence. They need to know the values and beliefs that you think should steer their decision making and action taking. After all, you'll want to be able to fit back in on your return.

You are permitted no long reports, however—just a one-page Credo Memo. Use all your responses to the preceding activities as resource material. Make some notes below. Record your Credo Memo on the following page, write it on a separate sheet of paper, or type it on your computer:

_____

_____

_____

_____

_____

_____

_____

_____

(***Note:*** Readers of *The Leadership Challenge* or those who have attended our workshop may already have prepared a credo statement. If so, please find it and look it over. Is your credo statement still accurate? Do you need to rewrite or edit it? Now is an opportunity to make changes.)

To: _____

Subject: Values That Should Guide Our Decisions and Actions

_____
_____
_____
_____
_____
_____
_____
_____
_____
_____
_____
_____
_____
_____
_____
_____

Acquire Competence

Before you can do the right things, you must know *how* to do them. Anyone who has ever dealt with an incompetent boss, or who can recall an incompetent teacher or other leader, will attest that, although that person may have occupied a leadership position, he or she was not credible. You do not have to know everything in order to do a job—after all, you can turn on a television without knowing how it was built—but you must have the knowledge, skills, and abilities to fulfill your role as leader and deliver on your promises. Do not commit to doing something that you have no capacity to perform—unless you are willing to do something about gaining that capacity!

Skill Assessment

Poor leadership is often the result of swashbuckling overconfidence accompanied by lack of ability. The credible leader is aware of his or her strengths as well as personal limitations.

What are your leadership strengths? What do you now do really well?

_____

_____

_____

_____

_____

What skills do you know you need to develop? How well can you execute what you value? What gives you pause or causes you to doubt yourself when confronted with a task or problem?

_____

_____

_____

_____

_____

_____

_____

Now, take another look at your top five values. For each of these, ask yourself, "To what extent do I possess the competence to deliver on this belief?" Ask: "In which of these do I most need to improve my knowledge, skills, and abilities?" Make note of them here.

I feel confident I have the competence to deliver on the following values:

_____

_____

_____

_____

_____

I need to improve on my competence around the following values:

_____

_____

_____

_____

_____

What are you doing about your leadership skills and your abilities to deliver on your values? What actions can you take to improve? Do you need to read a book or manual, find a mentor, watch someone else, or take a course? Write your ideas for development here:

_____

_____

_____

_____

_____

_____

One of the tools that is available to you is the *Leadership Practices Inventory* by Jim Kouzes and Barry Posner. It assesses the extent to which you now engage in The Five Practices of Exemplary Leadership®. You may find it useful to complete this assessment as a way of answering the questions about your leadership strengths and areas for improvement. You will find it on our website, www.leadershipchallenge.com.

Constant Improvement

One of the challenges with "learning" is that we don't always recognize when we're doing it. If you want, for example, to wallpaper your kitchen but don't know how, you might rent a video, buy a book, or attend a workshop at a home improvement store. But you probably don't think of yourself as "a motivated self-directed learner." You have a problem and figure out how to solve it. Try to take a few moments each day to reflect on what you have learned that day. Send yourself an auto-email at 5 P.M. each day that says, "What have you learned today?" Make it a habit to articulate your learning. If you haven't learned anything at all, then that should send a message that you need to change your activities so that you do learn something every day.

How valuable are you—to your constituents, to your customers or clients, to your stakeholders, and to your colleagues in the organization? To what extent do you actually have the capabilities to do what you say you will do? Where you lack the necessary competence, are you willing to acquire new knowledge and skills? How will you go about doing that? If time is short and the demand is immediate, what will you do to find someone better prepared for the job at hand?

_____

_____

_____

_____

_____

_____

_____

Debrief Experiences

The need for reflection, and setting aside time for it, tend to be lost as you finish one thing and quickly move on to another. It is critical to examine and learn from past actions. Review every project, big or small—each success as well as every single failure. Each work assignment is a chance to accomplish something and an opportunity to learn more about yourself and the values you and your constituents consider important. But to learn from these experiences, you must take the time to do so. The "Experiential Learning Model"[2] is one very useful debriefing guide. It includes these five dimensions:

1. *Experience:* First, focus on the project, task, or activity in which you have been engaged. Make sure that everyone has a common experience to use as the basis for discussion.

2. *Publish:* Next, ask, "What happened to me during this experience? What were my feelings, reactions, and observations?" Make sure that everyone has the opportunity to share his or her personal observations and record the raw data for later review.

3. *Process:* Together, look over the individual reactions and see whether you can find any repeated patterns, common themes, and trends. Make note of these recurring dynamics.

4. *Generalize:* Make generalizations and inferences from the common themes. What fundamental principles might be at work here? Find ways to extend what you have learned beyond the specific project so that you can make use of the lessons in planning and executing future assignments.

5. *Apply:* Apply the new lessons you have learned to the next project and start the experiential learning cycle over again.

This process can certainly be applied to personal projects; however, debriefings are most effective when done in a team setting with all the key participants in a project.

Believe You Can Do It

Self-confidence is not the same as competence. Knowing you can do something and believing that in a given situation you can use that competence to achieve your goals are different mindsets. Your belief in your own abilities is known as *self-efficacy.* Your self-efficacy affects your motivation, your persistence, your initiative, and, ultimately, your success. If you don't believe you can meet the challenge of a particular problem, then you probably won't— and you have little credibility for leading others in it.

Think self-efficacy doesn't matter?

Put a trash can on the floor about 8 feet from your chair. Take a piece of scrap paper, crumple it into a ball, and toss it into the trash can. Did you think you would make it? What impact did your thinking have on your confidence? Do you want to try again? Why?

Move 5 feet from the trash can and try again. Did you make it? Did you believe you would or that you would not? Did the difference in distance change how you felt about your chances of succeeding? Did your belief affect your chance of succeeding?

Putting the ball into the trash can—or not—likely affected your belief that you could do it again, and it affected your motivation as to whether you even wanted to try. If our self-efficacy can have this kind of impact on throwing a piece of paper across a room, what are the implications for tasks that matter?

In working to increase self-efficacy, the point isn't to become great at throwing paper balls—that's competence. Increasing self-efficacy means developing awareness of the way our thinking patterns can affect performance, recognizing the influence feelings can have on that performance, and working to manage or overcome things that may be having a negative impact.

Create a Personal Development Plan

You need to take charge of your own work life. You are responsible for your own development; you must not rely entirely on someone in human resources or in senior management. You must make a plan, give some focus to your development, and get on with it. That's clearly what the most effective leaders do.

Begin by auditing your present skills and abilities. Identify the specific job-related competencies you need to master in order to lead your constituents.

How do your abilities compare to what the situation, role, and tasks require?

_____

_____

_____

How well can you execute what you say you value? Where are there gaps? What specific knowledge, skills, and abilities do you have that will enable you to succeed in this environment?

_____

_____

_____

_____

_____

_____

Which knowledge, skills, and abilities do you need to acquire? What experiences do you need to sharpen these competencies?

_____

_____

_____

_____

_____

_____

Who is the very best in the world in your field, and how do you compare to that person? What can you do to become the best?

_____

_____

_____

_____

_____

Would your constituents respond to these questions in the same way?

_____

Be sure that your plan includes specific goals and activities in which you can immerse yourself. For example, because practice is one of the most significant contributors to self-confidence, include activities for practicing leadership basics—Modeling, Inspiring, Challenging, Enabling, and Encouraging—daily, just as a musician practices the scales. What is your development plan?

_____

_____

_____

_____

_____

_____

_____

_____

Ask for coaching from a colleague who has mastered the skill you are working on improving. Measure and ask for feedback on your progress (for example, utilizing the *Leadership Practices Inventory*). As you practice, ask others to give you constructive reactions to your performance. Knowing how far you have gone in your quest to improve is very important to building self-confidence.

Also, practice in the company of people who are interested in your being successful. Finally, pay attention to what is happening as you engage in the activities. Make sure that you learn to enjoy the immediate experience.

Sum It Up as Character

Credo, competence, and confidence are the contents of character, the things that give meaning to people.

What level of trust and confidence do you have in your own ability to competently meet the specific leadership challenges that confront your organization? What will you do to increase your self-efficacy: mastery experiences, observing role models, social support and encouragement, reinterpreting personal stress, something else? What will you do to structure conditions for success and surround yourself with supportive people?

_____

_____

_____

_____

_____

Your Leadership Legacy

In our workshops and university classes, we ask participants these questions:

Are you here to do something, or are you here for something to do? If you are here to do something, what is it? What will be your legacy?

How would you answer these questions for yourself? Take the time to do that by completing the activity on the following page.

"Leadership 2020"

Imagine that it's the year 2020, and you are attending a ceremony honoring you as the "Leader of the Year." One after another, colleagues and co-workers, members of your family, and good friends take the stage and talk about your leadership and how you have made a positive difference in their lives. What do you hope they will say about you? How do you hope you are remembered on that day?

Record your thoughts using the following L.I.F.E. themes:

Lessons: What vital *lessons* do you hope others will say you have passed on? (For example, "She taught me how to face adversity with grace and determination." "He taught me what it means to be a coach.")

_____

_____

_____

_____

_____

_____

Ideals: For what *ideals*—values, principles, and ethical standards—do you hope people will say you stood for? (For example, "She stood for freedom and justice." "He believed in always telling the truth, even when it wasn't what people wanted to hear.")

_____

_____

_____

_____

_____

_____

_____

Feelings: What *feelings* do you hope people will say they have/had when being with you or when thinking about you? (For example, "She always made me feel I was capable of doing the impossible." "He made me feel significant.")

_____

_____

_____

_____

_____

_____

Expressions: What lasting *expressions* or contributions—tangible and intangible—will people say that you leave to them and to others yet to come? (For example, "She is really the one who built this agency." "His dedication to others lives on in those homes that he helped to build every Saturday as he gave his time to Habitat for Humanity.")

_____

_____

_____

_____

_____

_____

_____

Theme: Review your L.I.F.E. responses above. As you review what you wrote, what is the central "theme"? What's at the core of the legacy you want to leave? (For example, "I want to be remembered for how I enabled people to learn and grow" or, "My central theme is innovation. I want to be remembered for bringing new and creative ideas to life and work.")

_____

_____

_____

_____

_____

_____

_____

Notes

1. The questions posed are based on the work of the original developers of the values clarification process; see L. Rath, M. Harmin, and S. Simon, *Values and Teaching* (Columbus, OH: Charles E. Merrill, 1966, p. 30). Also see S. Simon, L. Howe, & H. Kirschenbaum, *Values Clarification* (New York: Warner Books, 1995) and H. Smith, *What Matters Most: The Power of Living Your Values* (New York: Simon & Shuster, 2001).

2. Jones, J. E. An Experiential Model. In *Reference Guide to Handbooks and Annuals* (San Francisco: Pfeiffer, 1999, p. 3).

CHAPTER FOUR

Discipline 2: Appreciate Constituents

Organizations with adaptive, performance-enhancing cultures outperform non-adaptive, unhealthy ones precisely because of their emphasis on attending to all of their constituencies—their customers, stockholders, and employees. Leaders who are only interested in their own agendas, their own advancement, and their own well-being will not be willingly followed.

In the last chapter, you worked on clarifying your values and beliefs, but leadership Is not just about you. Leadership is a *relationship between you and your constituents*, and only by being constituent-oriented can you ultimately become trustworthy. When you appreciate and pay attention to others, you demonstrate that they are important to you, that their input and ideas are valued, and that you trust them.

Shift Focus from Self to Others Through Values

To begin to shift your focus, you must try to understand and appreciate the values and aspirations of your constituents. Respond to each item below using the scale provided.

To what extent do you truly understand and appreciate . . .

Your own personal values?

1	2	3	4	5
Not at All	Only a Little	Moderately	To a Great Extent	Completely

The values of your direct reports?

1	2	3	4	5
Not at All	Only a Little	Moderately	To a Great Extent	Completely

The values of your manager?

1	2	3	4	5
Not at All	Only a Little	Moderately	To a Great Extent	Completely

The values of your peers?

1	2	3	4	5
Not at All	Only a Little	Moderately	To a Great Extent	Completely

The values of your key outside business partners?

1	2	3	4	5
Not at All	Only a Little	Moderately	To a Great Extent	Completely

Whose values do you know the best? Whose do you know least well?

_____

_____

_____

_____

Write down the values that you believe are most important to those whose values you say you understand.

_____

_____

_____

_____

Make sure you take some time to have a conversation with people about their values.

What does this quick look at your understanding of others' values tell you, particularly as it compares to your understanding of yourself and your own values?

_____

_____

_____

_____

What can you do to gain a better understanding of others' values, dreams, aims, and aspirations?

_____

_____

_____

_____

Put those actions on your agenda for the next couple of weeks.

We've found that sometimes values shift over time. For example, our most recent research tells us that today, as compared to twenty years ago, family is reported to be a more important source of life satisfaction than one's career is. These kinds of shifts can happen as organizations become more global and diverse. What changes in values have you noticed in your workplace over the last few years? What do you think these changes are due to?

_____

_____

_____

_____

Quick Question: Name three work-related instances in the past week in which you have put someone else first.

_____

_____

_____

Learn About Others and About How Diversity Enriches Performance

Define "diversity" as you understand it. Is your definition broad (with multiple dimensions and categories) or narrow (focused and specific)?

_____

_____

_____

What do you do to foster good working relationships between people with differences in gender, age, ethnic, and/or racial backgrounds? What part do you play in creating a climate in which there is a strong sense that each person values and affirms the other, that each party is the other's supporter and admirer? What needs to change for this to be true?

_____

_____

_____

_____

_____

_____

_____

What Do You Really Know About Your Constituents?

Choose any three constituents (or more) and answer the following questions about each:

Level 1: Basic Knowledge

What do you know about these three people personally? What are their hobbies? Do they have families? Do they have children, and, if so, what are their approximate ages? What's their favorite type of book, movie, or music? What's their favorite type of food? What other basic information do you know about them as people?

Constituent 1 (Name:_____)

_____

_____

_____

Constituent 2 (Name:_____)

_____

_____

_____

Constituent 3 (Name: _____)

_____

_____

_____

Level 2: Work Knowledge

How did the people you listed above get into their line of work? What other jobs have they held? What tasks to they especially like or dislike? What skill do they have that they feel is underutilized? What role do they play in the work group/team? How do they feel about their lives, this workplace, the general state of the world, and so forth?

Constituent 1

_____

_____

_____

Constituent 2

_____

_____

_____

Constituent 3

_____

_____

_____

Level 3: What Do Your Constituents Want? What Is Important to Them?

It is sometimes difficult for leaders to understand that others may not share the same goals and aspirations as they do. Some people do not want to be leaders or managers; some prefer family or personal time over salary increases;

some need to feel a strong sense of personal power without necessarily needing to control or attempt to influence others. Think of the three constituents you wrote about above. Read over the list below of needs that work can help to fulfill. On a scale of 1 to 5 (where 1 = low and 5 = high) rate yourself, then rate each of those constituents. Where are there large differences? How can you help to meet *their* needs and wants?

Needs	*Myself*	*Constituent 1*	*Constituent 2*	*Constituent 3*
Accomplishment	_____	_____	_____	_____
Power	_____	_____	_____	_____
Recognition	_____	_____	_____	_____
Responsibility	_____	_____	_____	_____
Security	_____	_____	_____	_____
Self-Expression	_____	_____	_____	_____

Did you discover gaps in your knowledge of constituents? What do you still need to learn?

Do You Appreciate Constituents?

When is the last time you shared credit? What were the specifics?

_____

_____

_____

Think of your immediate constituents. What is one thing each has contributed in the past month? Articulate it in specific terms. Did you tell each person that you noticed and valued his or her contributions?

_____

_____

_____

_____

Begin Appreciation with Listening

Listening helps to show others that you respect them and consider them worthwhile. How often do you reach out to others, to ask what they're doing or feeling, or to ask for (and act on) their feedback?

_____

_____

_____

_____

_____

_____

Listening Self-Assessment*

To help you start to be more aware of your listening habits, complete the following listening self-evaluation. For each of the items, put an X in the appropriate column.

Communicating Knowledge and Attitudes	Most of the Time	Frequently	Occasionally	Almost Never
Do you . . .				
1. Tune out people who say something you don't agree with or don't want to hear?	————	————	————	————
2. Concentrate on what is being said, even if you are not really interested?	————	————	————	————
3. Assume you know what the talker is going to say and stop listening?	————	————	————	————
4. Repeat in your own words what the talker has just said?	————	————	————	————
5. Listen to the other person's viewpoint, even if it differs from yours?	————	————	————	————

*From Madelyn Burley Allen. (1995). *Listening: The Forgotten Skill: A Self-Teaching Guide, Second Edition*. Hoboken, NJ: John Wiley & Sons. Reprinted with permission of John Wiley & Sons, Inc.

Communicating Knowledge and Attitudes	Most of the Time	Frequently	Occasionally	Almost Never
6. Learn something from each person you meet, even if it is ever so slight?	————	————	————	————
7. Find out what words mean when they are used in ways not familiar to you?	————	————	————	————
8. Form a rebuttal in your head while the speaker is talking?	————	————	————	————
9. Give the appearance of listening when you aren't?	————	————	————	————
10. Daydream while the speaker is talking?	————	————	————	————
11. LIsten to the whole message—what the talker is saying verbally and nonverbally?	————	————	————	————
12. Recognize that words don't mean exactly the same thing to different people?	————	————	————	————
13. Listen to only what you want to hear, blotting out the talker's whole message?	————	————	————	————
14. Look at the person who is talking?	————	————	————	————

Communicating Knowledge and Attitudes	Most of the Time	Frequently	Occasionally	Almost Never
15. Concentrate on the talker's meaning rather than how he or she looks?	————	————	————	————
16. Know which words and phrases you respond to emotionally?	————	————	————	————
17. Think about how the other person might react to what you say?	————	————	————	————
18. Plan the best time to say what you want to say?	————	————	————	————
19. Think about how the other person might react to what you say?	————	————	————	————
20. Consider the best way to make your communication (written, spoken, phone, bulletin board, memo, etc.) work?	————	————	————	————
21. Think about what kind of person you're talking to (worried, hostile, disinterested, rushed, shy, stubborn, impatient, etc.)?	————	————	————	————
22. Interrupt the speaker while he or she is still talking?	————	————	————	————
23. Think, "I assumed he or she would know that"?	————	————	————	————

Communicating Knowledge and Attitudes	Most of the Time	Frequently	Occasionally	Almost Never
24. Allow the talker to vent negative feelings toward you without becoming defensive?	————	————	————	————
25. Practice regularly to increase your listening efficiency?	————	————	————	————
26. Take notes when necessary to help you to remember what was said?	————	————	————	————
27. Hear noises without being distracted by them?	————	————	————	————
28. Listen to the talker without judging or criticizing?	————	————	————	————
29. Restate instructions and messages to be sure you understand correctly?	————	————	————	————
30. Paraphrase what you believe the talker is feeling?	————	————	————	————

Scoring

Take the responses you checked previously and transfer your scores by circling the number that matches the frequency (most of the time, frequently, etc.) you checked on each of the thirty items of the self-evaluation.

For example: If you put an X under "frequently" for Number 1, you would circle 2 in the "frequently" column in the table below.

Then add the circled scores in each of the columns and write the sums on the Totals lines.

Item Number	Most of the Time	Frequently	Occasionally	Almost Never
1.	1	2	3	4
2.	4	3	2	1
3.	1	2	3	4
4.	4	3	2	1
5.	4	3	2	1
6.	4	3	2	1
7.	4	3	2	1
8.	1	2	3	4
9.	1	2	3	4
10.	1	2	3	4
11.	4	3	2	1
12.	4	3	2	1
13.	1	2	3	4
14.	4	3	2	1

15.	4	3	2	1
16.	4	3	2	1
17.	4	3	2	1
18.	4	3	2	1
19.	4	3	2	1
20.	4	3	2	1
21.	1	2	3	4
22.	1	2	3	4
23.	1	2	3	4
24.	4	3	2	1
25.	4	3	2	1
26.	4	3	2	1
27.	4	3	2	1
28.	4	3	2	1
29.	4	3	2	1
30.	4	3	2	1
Totals				

Grand Total (sum each of the column totals to reach a grand total): _____

Scoring

110 to 120   Superior

90 to 109   Above Average

88 to 98   Average

77 to 87   Fair

Action Plan

Reexamine your responses to the thirty items. What items would you like to improve upon? Pick three, and answer each of the following questions.

What I want to do to improve my listening skills:

_____

_____

_____

At work, improving my listening skills will

_____

_____

_____

_____

In my personal life, improving my listening skills will

_____

_____

_____

_____

Listening is not just about sitting down and talking one-on-one. It means walking around. It means sitting quietly in a meeting. It means hitting the road. It may mean learning another language. You can't listen from reading reports or hearing something secondhand. What do people have to do to reach you? Does everything have to go through an administrative assistant? If so, do you counter that by occasionally walking around? And remember, listening is learning—approach with a learning stance, and be willing to hear.

Can't always be in the same place as constituents? New technologies like Skype, web conferencing, Google Talk, and iPhone's Face Time can let you talk with constituents via real-time video. New social media tools like Facebook, Twitter, and LinkedIn can help you "listen." Does your company have blogs for sharing information? Do employees have Facebook groups for bridging distance? Leaders can use social media tools to ask questions, monitor keywords, and make themselves more available to employees, customers, and other constituents. (If you're concerned about what people will say on social media platforms, well, that points to another, and bigger, problem.)

Stretch

Think of a few topics on which you have a strong opinion, perhaps even something tied to a core value. For instance, consider your views on capital punishment, drug use and abuse, 21st century parenting, foreign policy, interracial or cross-religion marriage, divorce, or prison reform. State to yourself the opposite point of view without using judgmental or biased terms. You don't have to change your mind about these matters; you just need to be able to state someone else's opinion about them without judging or diminishing the other person.

When listening to another, it is important that you really *listen*. Don't spend time rehearsing your response, looking only for points on which you agree or disagree, or allowing yourself to become defensive. If you have been trained in listening skills—such as "active listening" techniques—be careful not to let the technique overwhelm the actual listening.

Promote Constructive Controversy

If you have paved the way for constituents to value one another and acknowledge differences, constructive controversy can provide an excellent means of collaborative problem solving. This is working toward a goal with different vehicles rather than one person or group trying to "win" or be right.

Ask yourself, In what ways do I suppress dissent or actively encourage it and demonstrate an appreciation of different points of view?

_____

_____

_____

_____

_____

How do I solicit constructive criticism and promote diverse expressions of opinion?

_____

_____

_____

_____

_____

What do I do to encourage balance and guard against polarization?

_____

_____

_____

_____

_____

What do I intend to do to learn to model the constructive controversy process?

_____

_____

_____

_____

_____

Safe Practice: You can practice the constructive controversy process with your constituents during a meeting or even as an individual assignment. Just ask them to play "devil's advocate": assign a problem or issue and ask each person to take a different position on it; everyone else must let the person speaking finish. This will have the collateral value of reinforcing listening and appreciation of diverse points of view. Try tossing out ideas such as: "Concerns for our customers should outweigh concerns for the bottom line," "Sometimes really difficult customers just need to be cut loose," or "It is not fair to implement a policy that doesn't apply to everyone in the organization. If the front-desk receptionist can't telework, then no one else should be allowed to either." Then move on to real issues of concern to your organization.

Engender Trust

The simple truth is that trusting other people encourages them to trust you, and distrusting others makes them more likely to distrust you. To be trusted, you have to extend yourself to your constituents by being available, by volunteering information, by sharing your personal experiences, and by making connections with their experiences and aspirations. You can help people trust you by the candor with which you talk about your actions. It's your behavior that earns trust, and we've found that there are a few key behaviors that influence how trustworthy people think you are. Being predictable, communicating clearly, treating promises seriously, being forthright and candid, and admitting mistakes are among the more important ones.

Do a brief assessment of your trustworthiness. For each of the following dimensions, indicate with an X where on the scale **you think other people see you**.

Other people see me as someone who:

Is predictable ———————————————————— Is erratic

Communicates clearly ———————————————— Communicates carelessly

Treats promises seriously —————————————— Treats promises lightly

Is forthright and candid ————————————— Is deceptive and dishonest

Readily admits mistakes ————————————— Is reluctant to admit mistakes

Remember, credibility is earned over time. Don't just consider one particular event in which you may have shown your credibility. Day by day, brick by brick, what message does your behavior send? What did the brief assessment above tell you about where you might want to focus some attention in building trust among your constituents?

CHAPTER FIVE

Discipline 3: Affirm Shared Values

You never know when a crisis or opportunity might rise in your organization or community and you will be called on to exercise leadership. But whenever you are, it's absolutely essential that you have a set of shared values to guide you and the confidence that others will respond positively to them. Leaders build consensus around shared values. Everyone in the organization needs to understand the fundamental beliefs that direct decisions and actions and the principles that are used to resolve the inevitable conflicts that arise in business and in life. Leaders build commitment to those values, and they help people to see themselves as part of a larger whole—as part of a community in which survival and success depend on a common understanding of purpose and principles.

Identify Your Constituents

Who are the people who must share a set of common values with you in order to get extraordinary things done? Your constituents could include your direct reports, your manager, peers, major suppliers, key customers, and other business partners. In the circles below, write names—one per circle—of your most important constituents. Keep this group in mind as you reflect on other questions and activities in this section of the workbook.

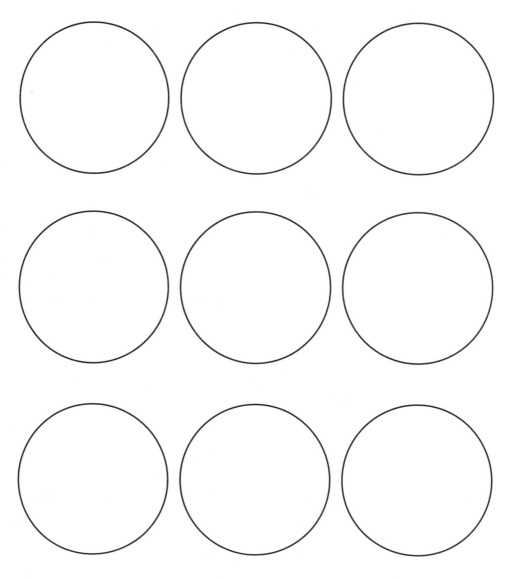

Find Common Ground

Get Together to Start Drafting Your Group's Credo

Soliciting people's ideas and listening to their concerns is critical. At the early stages of finding common ground, look for feedback; the start of the process is not the time for yes-or-no decisions. Ask such questions as "What interests of yours are not well represented?" "In what respect is it not fair?" "How would you improve upon it?" If people resist giving you their ideas or giving you feedback on yours, try to involve them by offering them a choice or list of alternatives. Once they select an alternative, it becomes their idea. The Chinese proverb, "Tell me, I may listen. Teach me, I may remember. Involve me, I will do it" is useful in this regard.

The best way to know what people think is to ask them. But what if you have lots of people? Send out a survey and find out what they think. One major worldwide clothing manufacturer distributed its survey to over 2,500 managers throughout the world, focusing specifically on the company's values, how well people understood them, supported and believed in them, and perceived that "living them" made a difference (that is, whether they were reflected in key actions and decisions).

What is your plan for gathering ideas about your organization's credo from constituents? (*Note:* Your "organization" might be the entire company, or it could be a region, division, business unit, or team. It all depends on your role in the organization and the unit you want to focus on. The same principles apply regardless of the size.) Will you have face-to-face conversations? Will you use a web-based tool like a Wiki to which everyone can add his or her thoughts? Conduct a large-scale survey? Write your draft plan here:

_____

_____

_____

_____

_____

_____

What will you ask?

_____

_____

_____

_____

_____

_____

Circulate a draft version of the credo in which you've incorporated everyone's ideas. Revise the draft and, if necessary, ask for more criticism. Gradually you will build consensus, because as people become involved they begin to think of the draft as their own. And it will be!

As noted in Chapter 1, leadership is a relationship. The more you know your constituents as individuals, the better you will understand their shared values. In talking with them, start asking questions like:

DISCIPLINE 3: AFFIRM SHARED VALUES

1. What are the three most important strengths or skills you are presently using on your job?

2. What aspects of your background, education, or work experience has been most valuable to you?

3. Which of your job tasks and activities do you enjoy the most?

4. What parts of your job do you find really interesting and energizing?

5. In your view, what are the most critical aspects of your job? How do you know this?

6. How much of what you really value is incorporated into the work you're currently doing?

7. On this job, which of your accomplishments are you the most proud of?

8. What would you like to be doing more of in your job? What would you like to be doing less? How does that fit with your career goals?

9. What ideas do you have for enriching your current job? How would it be possible for us to work together on that?

10. What are the important values and beliefs that you think should guide the decisions and actions we take in this organization?

Conduct "Stay" Interviews

Many businesses conduct exit interviews when employees leave the organization, but few conduct "stay" interviews. Occasionally ask constituents—particularly those who have been with the company for several years—why they stay. Their answers may reveal a good deal about their values and their perceptions of leaders and accomplishments. Try doing the same with clients and customers.

Make Sure There Is Agreement Around Values

On-the-Job Activity

In a staff meeting, or on a bulletin board or other public place, provide a list of values your group holds in common.

1. Ask constituents to anonymously select from the list of values their top five to seven. (An option you can consider is to use *The Leadership Challenge Workshop Values Cards*.[1] This is a fun and thoughtful way to sort through values and create a lively discussion around them.) Once they have selected their personal values, ask your constituents to write their values on a sticky-back note or index card, one value per note.

2. Next, ask constituents to either place their values cards or sticky-back notes in a pile (if in a group setting) or on the bulletin board (if in a public area). This activity can be done online via your company wiki or website, or as a standalone with an online sticky-note tool such as Linoit or Zapit.[2]

3. Now, arrange the values notes into categories around particular themes, such as "accomplishment" or "appreciation." Cluster together values words that are similar to each other; for example, "teamwork" and "collaboration" belong in the same set. The values that are likely to be shared are those for which there are more notes in the piles. Based on the number of times a value is mentioned, determine the five to seven most important clusters of "shared values." This creates a powerful visual, as people can see commonalities with their colleagues.

4. Use this activity as a shared values discussion-starter. It may also be a starting place for a new company mission or vision statement. Focus on understanding what values are truly shared. Identify the level of

agreement. Work with the group to clarify what is vital to alignment and determine what is secondary.

Another technique for exploring agreement is to connect values with "Why." In *Credibility* Chapter 3, several studies are described that found the only teacher behavior that was effective in raising the moral reasoning of school children was the Socratic question, "Why?"[3] A similar case can be made for leaders and their constituents. So for each of the core values that your team selects in the above activity, ask them to answer the question: "Why is this important to us?" Their responses will help to clarify the rationale for the value as well as provide guidance on how it can be used to guide actions and decisions. For example, in its "Values Statement," one Fortune 50 most-admired company listed its key values along with statements about what each value means and why it is important. Consider the business value of being "lean." What it means is "reduce tasks and the people required to do them." Why is lean a value? It is "critical to developing work cost leadership."

The importance of certain values may seem self-evident. But commitment is facilitated when you can help people know that the values are not just their own, individually, but are shared by others, endorsed, and put into practice by the organization. Moreover, providing a rationale for the value helps people to remember and internalize it. In addition, this level of understanding enables them to apply the "logic" of that value to new and different situations, promoting a consistency in the interpretation and enactment of values.

Try including some of your relevant customers, suppliers, vendors, and even shareholders in your values discussions. Present hypothetical situations involving value dilemmas and ask people to consider what actions they would take in these cases. Have them link their proposed actions back to key values. Take a recent organizational or team decision and analyze it in terms of agreement with shared values.

Create a Cooperative Community

It is important that people feel they are part of a larger whole—that the sum of the community is greater than its parts. "Community" doesn't mean that everyone needs to be best friends, but that they have a shared sense of values and purpose. Community can't be forced, but it can be encouraged and nurtured. And people must feel there is something in it for them, a reason for them to participate in the community.

In order for people to perceive themselves as part of a community, they must believe that their goals are cooperative and that they share a common purpose. Only then will people make their co-workers' problems their own and solve them together. For constituents in the United States, in the wake of 9/11 and the challenges of the economy in the early 21st century, people more than ever need to feel the workplace is safe and that they belong and are supported.

Ask yourself:

What actions have I taken with constituents to determine our shared values?

_____

_____

_____

To what extent have others actively participated?

_____

_____

_____

What could I do differently to ensure their contribution to and participation in developing our sense of collective purpose and meaning?

_____

_____

_____

How committed are we all to our values and purpose? What could I do differently?

_____

_____

_____

To what extent do constituents identify with each other? That is, to what extent do they see themselves as part of a unified community?

_____

_____

_____

What am I doing to build a work community?

_____

_____

_____

Is the community inclusive? Is anyone isolated? Is anyone marginalized? Why? What will I do to change that? How can I foster inclusion?

_____

_____

_____

_____

To what extent have I structured cooperative goals?

_____

_____

_____

_____

What actions have I taken to foster collaboration and team accountability?

_____

_____

_____

_____

How can I allow the community to make decisions, or do I have to be willing to delegate?

_____

_____

_____

_____

What have I done to express expectations of trusting relationships on the team? How have I encouraged constituents to deal openly with problems and conflicts? What needs to change?

_____

_____

_____

Pay attention: Have your constituents already built a community for themselves? How can you become a part of it rather than an interloper?

Advocate Cooperation and Build Consensus

Structure Cooperative Goals

It is essential for the creation of a "team" that people perceive that they are interconnected and that they have cooperative goals. There are several strategies you can use for ensuring that goals are cooperative.[4] For instance, discuss the team's vision and have members explore how the vision can be best achieved by everyone working together. Have the team analyze the factors critical to achieving their vision. Have the team members identify what needs to be done, determine priorities, resolve differences, and assign people to various roles and responsibilities.

What are your ideas for working toward cooperative goals?

_____

_____

_____

_____

_____

_____

_____

Or keep track of the team's productivity by having everyone average his or her individual output to form a group average for some specified period (perhaps weekly). In this latter case, people can see that they are responsible for keeping their own output up and for helping others to improve theirs. Another strategy is to promote group learning. Have everyone on the team teach another individual about his or her job or task responsibilities. Encourage cross-functional and interdisciplinary learning.

Reinforce Shared Values Through Organizational Systems

Shared values need to be more than a nicely lettered item in a pretty frame. What do your organizational systems say? Do the daily processes and organizational structure send messages that strengthen the sense of shared values?

Recruitment/Hiring: Are values and shared goals apparent in recruiting materials? Does the organization work to attract and hire those with similar values, or does it just fill jobs? Does the organization look for people who can become successful members of the community, or just enact work roles? What could be done to more closely tie the recruitment and hiring processes to shared values?

_____

_____

_____

Orientation: How are new hires brought on-board and into the community? For example, does someone sit them down and tell them about the company dress code? The first few days on the job are critical, and the messages sent then will affect the new hire's attitude toward his or her work and the organization. What can be put into place to help new hires more quickly find a place in the community? What would help to convey a sense of shared values, rather than just rules for the workplace?

_____

_____

_____

_____

Artifact Review: Take a look at your organization's website, marketing materials, bulletin boards, brochures, Facebook pages, help-wanted postings, and advertising. Google your organization. What messages are being sent? Are they congruent with your stated values? Remember, these items may be where a potential new hire first hears about you and your organization. What might he or she think before even applying for the job?

_____

_____

_____

Training: Do employees fall victim to the "Dilbert Paradox"—they are hired for their talents, but then no investment is made in helping them develop? Many companies invest time in helping employees tie work behaviors to shared values and traditions. Are you doing this? What could be done to begin or to strengthen training in regard to shared values?

_____

_____

_____

_____

_____

Recognitions: Rewards and recognitions send powerful signals to people about what's important to you and to the organization. Whether it's a tangible reward or an informal "thank you," credible leaders make sure there's a clear link between recognition and the shared values of the organization. When you recognize someone, are you always explicit about that connection? How are you doing this now? What more can you do to link values with reward and recognition?

_____

_____

_____

_____

_____

Promotions: Of all the things that happen within an organization, perhaps nothing sends stronger, more public messages than decisions about promotions. Is advancement tied only to technical skill or, worse, to political connections? Or are promotional considerations tied to employees' visible efforts to "walk the talk" of the organization's values as well as their technical ability? Think about the last few promotions in your organization. What message did they send? Is there anything that needs rethinking in the future in regard to promotions and promotional opportunities?

_____

_____

_____

_____

Talk the Walk

Be an Enthusiastic Spokesperson for Shared Values

You need to speak enthusiastically about shared values. Find opportunities to talk about your common purpose and the importance of community. Let people know that everyone is in this together and that, while what each person does is important and that his or her contributions make a difference, the payoff is not for the individual but for everyone's collective accomplishments. When their leader speaks with passion about shared beliefs, it fills people with energy and enthusiasm. Your task is to keep people focused by continually, and publicly, affirming shared values.

Speaking out on behalf of shared values contributes to creating community. This finding is underscored by researchers who randomly stopped students walking across a college campus and asked them what they thought about a much a publicized incident of an African-American student receiving hate mail. Before the subject could respond, however, a confederate of the researchers would come up and answer. One response was something like, "Well, he must have done something to deserve it." The confederate's alternate response was something like, "There's no place for that kind of behavior on our campus." As you might expect, the subject's response was more often than not just like the confederate's.[5] This study illustrates clearly the importance of "affirming" and why leaders must speak out strongly on behalf of values and persuade others to do the same.

Shared Values Don't Equal Shared Skills

Establish a Sunset Statute for Your Credo

Tom Peters, noted commentator on organizational excellence, has remarked that "all good ideas are eventually oversold. Corporate vision and values are no exception." He's openly skeptical of organizations being able to review and update visions and values regularly and suggests "there ought to be a 'values sunset statute'—throw out a third of your values every five years, or burn the lot and start over every ten years."[6] Perhaps there is some merit in his suggestion. Rather than waiting for chance to do this or circumstance to require it, consider the practice of systematically reviewing and revising, as necessary, your team's credo. Consider applying the concept of zero-base budgeting to your value and vision. After all, many people will probably have left your group since the original inception of your shared values statement, and some of the new people will rightfully feel they have not been included in this part of your organizational history. While certain values will endure, there will be changes (some slight and some considerable), and the process of reviewing and prioritizing can only reinforce your team's unity of purpose and commitment to their shared values.

What is the expected lifespan or "sunset statute" for your group credo?

_____

_____

_____

In working to develop shared values and nurture a community in which they can flourish, it is important to remember that values are not just buzz-words on a poster. Shared values should drive behavior and serve as a guide for constituents as they deal with day-to-day issues, decisions, and other elements of enacting their work. As a leader, you serve a critical role in helping the group define and live by the values you all share.

Notes

1. For information on ordering Values Cards, visit www.leadershipchallenge .com; click on the Products link and then the Training Materials link. For more information, email leadership@wiley.com.
2. There are a number of online sticky-note tools, including those found at http://www.en.linoit.com/ and http://www.zapits.com/.
3. For example, see Colby, A., Kohlberg, L., Fenton, E., Speicher-Durbin, B., & Lieberman, M. (1997). "Secondary School Moral Discussion Programmes Led by Social Studies Teachers." *The Journal of Moral Education*, 6(2), 90–111.

4. For example, see Cloke, K., Goldsmith, J., & Bennis, W. (2005). *Resolving Conflicts at Work: Eight Strategies for Everyone on the Job.* San Francisco: Jossey-Bass; and Runde, C., & Flanagan, T. (2010). *Developing Your Conflict Competence: A Hands-On Guide for Leaders, Managers, Facilitators, and Teams.* San Francisco: Jossey-Bass..

5. Blanchard, F. A., Lilly, T., & Vaughn, L. A. (1991, March). "Reducing the Expression of Racial Prejudice." *Psychological Science*, *2*(2), 101–105.

6. Peters, T. J. (1991, October 12). "When Values Become Blinders." *San Jose Mercury News*, p. D2.

CHAPTER SIX

Discipline 4: Develop Capacity

People can't do what they say they will do if they don't know how. Credible leaders know that they have to continuously develop the capacity of their constituents to put shared values into practice. When individuals, teams, departments, and organizations are better able to perform their jobs and keep their promises, not only are their reputations enhanced, but the leader's credibility also grows. As a leader, in order to grow your own asset base, you have to invest in others. Credible leaders provide the resources and other organizational supports that enable constituents to put their abilities to constructive use.

The Five Cs

There are five essentials for developing capacity so that everyone can act in a free and responsible way. Think of them as the "Five Cs":

1. *Competence:* credible leaders invest in developing people's skills and abilities to deliver on shared values.

2. *Choice:* credible leaders enhance an ownership mindset by making sure people have choices about how they implement shared values.

3. ***Confidence:*** credible leaders strengthen people's belief in their own abilities to act on shared values—in their sense of personal efficacy.

4. ***Climate:*** credible leaders create a climate conducive to continuous learning, especially learning from inevitable mistakes.

5. ***Communication:*** credible leaders readily share information and provide feedback so that people always know what's going on and how they are doing.

Take a moment to assess how you are doing on each of these five essentials of developing capacity. In completing this assessment, refer back to the list of shared values you developed in Chapter 5. For purposes of this activity, there's space to assess yourself on two of your shared values, but you should consider doing this for all of them. Record a shared value on the line provided, and then assess yourself in the context of that value.

Shared Value 1: _____

To what extent are you doing each of the following with regard to this value? Circle the appropriate response using the following scale:

	To a small extent	To some extent	To a moderate extent	To a great extent	To a very great extent
1. Building Competence	1	2	3	4	5
2. Offering Choices	1	2	3	4	5
3. Fostering Confidence	1	2	3	4	5
4. Creating a Learning Climate	1	2	3	4	5
5. Communicating Information	1	2	3	4	5

Shared Value 2: _____

To what extent are you doing each of the following with regard to this value? Circle the appropriate response using the following scale:

	To a small extent	To some extent	To a moderate extent	To a great extent	To a very great extent
1. Building Competence	1	2	3	4	5
2. Offering Choices	1	2	3	4	5
3. Fostering Confidence	1	2	3	4	5
4. Creating a Learning Climate	1	2	3	4	5
5. Communicating Information	1	2	3	4	5

Based on the assessment you have just completed, what areas need improvement? Why do you feel these areas are low? For instance, are you hesitant to offer choices? Are you uncomfortable communicating and sharing information? What are your ideas for improving in these areas? Try to be specific.

_____

_____

_____

_____

_____

In supporting the five Cs of competence, choice, confidence, climate, and communication, you may find that you have the skills, but lack the necessary commitment. Giving your constituents choice will involve some risk on your part. Developing competence may involve rearranging schedules while a constituent attends training. Some actions important to supporting the five Cs are listed below. Consider the degree to which you feel committed to each, and reflect on what might strengthen your level of commitment.

- Making sure constituents feel engaged by their work
- Providing the resources and support to enable them to put their abilities to constructive use
- Encouraging experimentation and risk taking
- Making it easy to learn from mistakes
- Enabling constituents to take responsibility and accountability for their actions
- Ensuring constituents have latitude and discretion in performing their work
- Helping people believe they can be successful
- Creating opportunities for small wins over time
- Keeping people informed about what is going on in the organization
- Giving feedback on how people are doing

Build Competence: Educate, Educate, Educate

As we discussed earlier, being competent is essential to being seen as credible. People won't believe in you if they don't think you have the skills and abilities to deliver on your promises. They may like you and they may agree with what you say, but if they're going to follow you they need to know you are capable

100

of getting the job done. The same is true for those you lead. The members of your organization also have to be seen as competent if their customers and business partners are going to believe in what they say. That's why it's so critical that you focus a lot of your attention on developing your own capacity as well as the capacity of all your constituents. None of you can do what you say if you don't know how, so a vital part of your leadership job is developing "know how." You have to educate, educate, educate.

Educate does not always mean a formal scheduled training event. Forward-thinking leaders recognize how and when real learning occurs, and it is generally not solely within the walls of a classroom. That may be where ideas germinate or where employees are provided with concepts for future performance, but people learn best about how to work effectively *in* work and *at* work as they go about their work. Learning comes during coaching from supervisors and mentors and conversations with co-workers, by asking questions, and often through trial and error—sometimes big errors!

Think about the three most significant learning experiences you have ever had. What were the circumstances? Where did they occur? Who else was involved? Did you realize at the time that you were *learning*?

1._____

_____

_____

_____

2._____

_____

_____

_____

3._____

_____

_____

_____

How can you create more learning experiences for yourself and for your constituents? How can you become, and encourage them to become, more mindful of their own learning?

_____

_____

_____

_____

_____

_____

Simple ways of providing education include:

- Offer flexible scheduling to allow employees time for educational and training endeavors.
- Offer tuition reimbursement or matching funding.
- Open up training opportunities: remove passwords and approvals for online programs; be sure constituents are aware of training programs and schedules.
- Work with constituents to write personal development plans and support them in following up on those plans.
- Encourage constituents to develop mentoring relationships with other leaders or someone in another work unit.

- Learn to be a better mentor: take advantage of mentor training opportunities for yourself.
- Others? Add your own ideas:

_____

_____

Developing People

For each item below, circle one rating indicating your view of how often you exhibit that behavior, where 1 = seldom and 5 = almost always.

	Seldom			Almost Always	
1. I take seriously my responsibility for coaching and mentoring others.	1	2	3	4	5
2. I invest adequate amounts of time on constituent development.	1	2	3	4	5
3. I'm committed to helping people from diverse segments of my constituent base.	1	2	3	4	5
4. I create opportunities for people to assess their leadership skills.	1	2	3	4	5
5. I help people take advantage of opportunities to learn new skills.	1	2	3	4	5
6. I look for ways to help others become more successful at their jobs.	1	2	3	4	5
7. I help people take advantage of opportunities for new experiences.	1	2	3	4	5
8. I ask the people I mentor to define their expectations.	1	2	3	4	5
9. I work with people to create mutually agreed-on development plans.	1	2	3	4	5

Given your responses to the above statements, what are the two or three that you think are your strengths in developing people as credible leaders?

_____

_____

_____

_____

_____

What do you think are your most important areas for improvement in developing people?

_____

_____

_____

_____

_____

Give some thought to individual constituents or constituent groups. What are some specific areas in which they could benefit from further learning and development? What are your ideas about specific training or other activities for supporting this learning? Repeat the activity as needed for all your constituents or constituent groups.

Constituent 1

_____

_____

_____

_____

Constituent 2

_____

_____

_____

_____

Constituent 3

_____

_____

_____

_____

Enrich People's Jobs

The content of many jobs is not particularly glamorous, and indeed every job has some amount of grunt work associated with it. Yet the most high-performing companies have been able to augment people's jobs so that employees understand that whatever they are doing makes a difference and they feel connected to the big picture. You can best liberate the leader within your constituents by understanding how the contextual factors of their jobs may contribute to lower feelings of personal effectiveness and reduced motivation. Typically, this happens when people perceive themselves as lacking control over their immediate situation or lacking the required capability, resources, or discretion needed to accomplish a task. The most common reasons are excessive bureaucracy, authoritarian supervisory styles, non-merit-based reward systems, and job design.[1] Here are some ideas for ways to address the area of job design:

- Make certain that people's jobs are designed so that they know what is expected of them, and provide sufficient training and technical support so that people can complete their assignments successfully.

- Enrich people's responsibilities so that they experience variety in their task assignments and opportunities to make meaningful decisions about how their work is accomplished. Create occasions for them to network with others in the organization (including both peers and senior managers).

- Involve everyone in programs, meetings, and decisions that have a direct impact on their job performance. When working on projects, let them handle planning, not just execution.

- Take a careful look at what your constituents are doing in their jobs and determine—with their input—where you could be enriching their positions and consequently fostering greater self-confidence.

- Give everyone a customer. That's a sixth "C" to add to our developing-capacity list (competence, confidence, choice, climate, and communications)—customers (or clients). Make certain everyone in your organization has a customer. Call this "customer focus" or whatever you want (retail bankers call it "relationship banking"), but do it today.

- List several constituents or constituent groups. Who are their "customers"?

Constituent 1

_____

_____

Constituent 2

_____

_____

Constituent 3

_____

_____

Make certain that whatever people are doing, they have another individual or group in mind that they are serving through their efforts. Otherwise, people will feel disconnected from their efforts and will find little reason to be as responsive as they could be. Having a customer enlarges people's understanding of what they do and also what the company overall does, and it typically puts each person in direct contact with other parts of the business.

Let Constituents Be the Teachers

The late Peter Drucker pointed out that "knowledge workers and service workers learn most when they teach."[2] He explained that the best way to improve productivity is to have people teach. So have one of your star salespeople present "the secret of my success" at the company's sales conference or have the top surgeon give a talk at the county medical society. School teachers have realized a similar principle: older children's learning can be enhanced by having them tutor younger students. In this process the learning of both parties is strengthened.

Take, for example, the case at one large multinational high-technology firm. Most people in their workforce were highly competent scientific and professional employees—but many had very little formal understanding of how businesses operate. A cross-functional group of employees was charged with determining what people needed to know in order to work effectively in a faster-paced and more self-directed work team environment. The first course they designed was around product flow. They made a video to explain how products move from one department to the next in the development, production, and distribution process. The next course, designed with the help of their cost accounting department, taught basic cost accounting to all employees. Another course dealt with production control for all employees. The courses were designed by the people who had questions about how things work and staffed by teachers (experienced personnel in that subject or department) as well as learners.

Don't forget that teaching can also be quite informal. A study by the Palo Alto Research Center (PARC) revealed, for example, that service personnel learn more of what they need to know about fixing copiers by swapping stories than they do from reading the company's manuals.[3] So instead of breaking up the gang by the water cooler, make opportunities for story-telling as teaching at informal get-togethers and loosely organized off-site meetings.

Offer Choices, Foster Ownership, and Foster Confidence

Credible leaders foster an ownership mindset by making sure people have choices about what they do. Providing people with choice gives them the freedom to use their judgment, their experience, and their education or training to do what is right.

To be a credible leader, you need to do everything you can to bolster self-efficacy and to foster greater self-confidence in others. Remember that how you react to mistakes can make all the difference in a constituent's confidence and belief that he or she will succeed.

It is important for leaders to convey their confidence in constituents. The work of Albert Bandura,[4] here encapsulated by Gio Valiante,[5] illustrates the role of self-efficacy in effective performance.

- Performances do not happen, we bring them about. People contribute to, not merely predict their performance.
- People who doubt their capabilities:
  - Shy away from difficult tasks
  - Give up quickly
  - Have low aspirations
  - Dwell on deficiencies, formidableness of tasks
  - Focus on adverse consequences of failure
  - *Thus, they undermine their efforts by:*
    - Diverting attention from effective thinking
    - Being slow to recover from setbacks
    - Falling easy victims to stress and depression

Can you think of someone you know who may have problems with low self-efficacy—including yourself? What behaviors and actions, or lack of action, do you see? What is the outcome?

_____

_____

_____

_____

People with a strong belief in their capabilities:

- Approach difficult tasks as challenges to be mastered (not threats to be avoided)
- Show interest in learning to do well
- Set challenging goals and maintain commitment to those goals
- Have high effort
- *Thus they*:
    - Think strategically
    - Attribute failure to insufficient effort
    - Quickly recover after failure
    - Reduce stress

Can you think of someone you would describe as having strong self-efficacy—including yourself? What behaviors and actions are exhibited? What are the results?

_____

_____

_____

_____

_____

_____

What can you do to strengthen confidence and self-efficacy among your constituents? What will be the benefits of doing this?

_____

_____

_____

_____

Create a Climate for Learning

Credible leaders create a climate in which learning is prized and rewarded. One place to begin creating a learning climate is for the leader to model the competencies they expect of others. Modeling is a powerful way to reinforce the skills that are prized in the organization.

Use Modeling to Develop Competencies

- Modeling is used in a wide variety of settings to develop intellectual, social, and behavioral competencies. The method that produces the best results includes three major elements: First, the appropriate skills are modeled to convey the basic competencies. Second, people receive guided practice under simulated conditions so they can perfect the skills. Third, they are helped to apply their newly learned skills in work conditions in ways that will bring them success.

- Determine the competencies you want to develop and then break complex skills down into sub-skills. Demonstrate, in-person or via video, the desired skill (or behavior) using many brief examples. Use role models that are similar to your audience (since having respected peers as

111

teachers is particularly effective). As people perfect their skills, especially new ones, provide informational feedback on how they are doing. Focus on the corrective changes that need to be made, rather than emphasizing what was wrong or flawed. Here's a hint: To practice being a "teacher," first try demonstrating, step-by-step, how to make a peanut butter and jelly sandwich. Or how to tie a necktie.

- Keep in mind that feedback should be given to build confidence in an individual's capabilities. This is achieved by calling attention to successes and improvements, while correcting deficiencies. Give people the opportunity to practice new skills, especially in situations in which they are likely to produce good results. Sufficient success using what they have learned is necessary so that they believe in themselves and in the value of behaving in new ways. Remember, the purpose of instruction is to support gains and not to expose inadequacy.

Share Information, Give Feedback

Credible leaders know that sharing information is critical in developing people's capacity and in building and sustaining credibility. When there's a high degree of transparency, and when information is easily available and accessible, people come to trust their leaders, their team members, and their organizations.

Share the Big Picture

Imagine that you have a 5,000-piece jigsaw puzzle. You dutifully hand out each and every piece to your constituents, and exhort: "Now you have all the resources you need to complete this project. Go to it!" What do you think they will say to you? How often have you been handed an assignment, given a budget, staff, and other materials without ever really knowing or understanding what it is that you are being asked to produce? People need to know what the picture on the puzzle box looks like. As an added benefit, by seeing the big picture, they typically also can easily see what the boundaries are so that they are aware of the constraints within which they have to operate in completing the puzzle (or project).

Ensure That Everyone Becomes Responsible

To build and sustain credibility, ensure that everyone is responsible for guiding the organization toward its future and maintaining alignment with values. Developing capacity is about building the skills, knowledge, and attitudes of the entire workforce at all levels to DWYSYWD.

A key component of effective performance, self-efficacy, and learning is the feeling that one is in control of one's own life. As a leader, try to focus on ways to empower those you lead to give them a sense of control in their own decisions and destinies.

Reflection: The Critical Questions You Must Ask Yourself

How willing are you to distribute leadership across the organization?
How committed are you to liberating the leader in everyone?
What needs to change?

Notes

1. Conger, J. A. (1989). "Leadership: The Art of Empowering Others." *The Academy of Management Executive, 3*(1), 17–24.

2. Drucker, P. F. (1991, November/December). "The New Productivity Challenge." *Harvard Business Review, 69,* 69–79.

3. Stewart, T. A. (1991, June 3). "Brainpower." *Fortune,* p. 50.

4. Bandura, A. (1986). *Social Foundations of Thought and Action: A Social-Cognitive Theory.* Englewood Cliffs, NJ: Prentice Hall, and *Self-Efficacy: The Exercise of Control* (1997). New York: Worth Publishers.

5. Valiante, G. at www.des.emory.edu/mfp/effbook2.html.

CHAPTER SEVEN

Discipline 5:
Serving a Purpose

Serving a purpose means that credible leaders put ahead of all else the guiding principles of the organization and of the people who have made it possible for them to lead. They strengthen credibility by demonstrating that they are not in it for themselves, but instead have the interests of the institution, department, or team and its constituents at heart. Their measure of success is whether their constituents grow and whether their constituents are more likely to become leaders in their own right.

The truth is that you either lead by example or you don't lead at all. Credible leaders walk the talk. They do what they say they will do, and they don't ask others to do something they wouldn't do themselves. Credible leaders hold themselves accountable to the same set of standards as they hold others.

In asking yourself, "Do I do what I say I will do?" reflect on how you spend your time. In what ways is your calendar an indicator of what you think is important? What do your everyday appointments and encounters say about your priorities? How can you change? One strategy for answering these questions is to conduct a personal audit.

Personal Audit

You can audit the alignment between your words and deeds along a number of dimensions. Below we have listed a few of the more important ones: your daily routines, the questions you ask, how you handle critical incidents, your communications, the rewards and recognitions you give. You can complete this audit by yourself or you can ask someone else to fill it out about you. But make sure if you take this audit that you are willing to set in motion changes that will realign your actions and behaviors to be more consistent with serving a purpose—otherwise you'll waste your own and everyone else's time and foster cynicism.

1. *Audit your daily routines.* Determine whether or not you are spending sufficient time on matters consistent with your shared values. Use your shared values as the basis for planning your weekly schedule. Let values be your guide, not old habits or the in-basket. Audit your daily calendar: How much time are you spending modeling shared values? How do your appointments contribute to communicating and reinforcing shared values? Look at the agenda for your meetings. What topics are discussed? Are the ones related to your shared values at the top?

_____

_____

_____

_____

_____

_____

2. *Audit your questions.* What questions do you typically ask in meetings, one-on-one, in telephone calls, and in interviews? How do these questions help you to clarify and gain commitment to shared values? Make a list of probing questions that correspond to each of your shared values.

_____

_____

_____

_____

_____

_____

_____

3. *Look at how you deal with critical incidents.* How did you respond to the most recent incident? To what extent did your actions teach lessons about the most important shared values? In your next interview, use your shared values as the basis for the questions. Whenever you start a new relationship with a supplier, begin by providing the supplier with a copy of the company credo. Talk about the kind of organization you are and explain that they should know this if they are going to be in business with you.

_____

_____

_____

_____

_____

_____

_____

4. ***Audit your internal memos, in-basket, and other communications.***
How are you using communications to foster commitment to shared values?
What percentage of your incoming and outgoing e-mail relates to shared
values? What percentage of your blogs, Facebook messages, or Twitter tweets
are about shared values? How much of the content of the stories that you
tell are about shared values? What might explain this? How might you bring
about better alignment?

_____

_____

_____

_____

_____

_____

5. ***Audit the rewards and recognitions that are being given out.*** Who's
being rewarded? Do these people exemplify best the values you want
to reinforce? When someone is recognized, do you clearly indicate
the value (or standard) on which the reward is based? How can you

118

influence other parts of the organization where values and rewards are not in alignment?

_____

_____

_____

_____

_____

_____

Summarize your observations by asking yourself these questions:

- By what actions do I show that I am not in this for myself, but have the interests of my organization and its constituents at heart?
- To what extent do I understand and act upon the principles of servant leadership?
- How do I show that one way I measure success is whether those I serve grow more capable, more autonomous, and more free?
- How have I established an atmosphere in which people feel comfortable about speaking up and telling the truth?

_____

_____

_____

_____

_____

_____

_____

Go First

Credible leaders are the first to do what has been agreed upon. In taking the first step, they provide tangible evidence of their commitment and are visible models of the kinds of behavior that are expected.

How have you shown your commitment to going first and setting a positive example of what you expect from others? Have you stepped in and made decisions on matters of principle? Taken a difficult stand? Put your career or safety on the line in the service of shared values?

_____

_____

_____

How have you illustrated consistency between words and deeds in the stories you've told, both about your own actions and about the actions of respected colleagues?

_____

_____

_____

How have you made yourself accessible and approachable?

_____

_____

_____

Are You Accountable?

Being credible means that you use the same standards and criteria for yourself that you apply to others. If customer service is important, find time to spend with customers. If your message is that "we're all in this together," then make certain your own actions reinforce this message. Simply put, the point is this: Don't ask anyone else to do something you are not willing to do yourself.

Collect data from your constituents regarding your leadership accountability. In a broader way, this is another strategy for keeping in touch. Consider asking such questions as:

- How are my actions consistent with the work we do?
- In your opinion, how capable am I of leading us toward greater excellence and opportunity?
- How have I helped you to achieve your personal goals?
- To what extent do you trust me with your plans to grow and develop?
- When have I been consistent with the values I communicate and the decisions I make? When does it appear that I have not been consistent?

_____

_____

_____

_____

_____

_____

_____

To ensure that all parties know their feedback will be taken seriously, make it public (while also respecting each person's confidentiality). Make it clear what this feedback means to you in terms of continuing, or taking, any new behaviors and actions.

Stay in Touch

To sustain credibility, you must stay in touch. You must continually listen and learn about your constituents and the organization's issues. Staying in touch also means that you remain approachable and gain feedback from a variety of sources, including across functions and levels.

A critical part of staying in touch is listening. And a critical part of listening is receiving bad news. Think about the last time a constituent brought you bad news. How did you respond? Did you thank him or her? Did you consider the greater good or your own self-interests? Did you talk with the constituent about implications, solutions, and corrections or mostly provide rationales and excuses?

_____
_____
_____
_____
_____
_____
_____
_____

What do you imagine was the effect of this interaction on that individual? What did you teach the person—to trust you or to hide bad news in the future?

_____
_____
_____
_____

Jane Bozarth recalls a time early in her career as an e-learning designer. She was in a newly created job with a new boss, and one Tuesday morning was launching her first big-scale online learning program to a large work group. Jane recalls that *everything* went wrong. Everything. Browsers didn't work, pages didn't load, and videos wouldn't play. The failure was frustrating—and public. Jane had no choice but to go to her new boss's office to apprise her of the situation. Her boss's response, in its entirety: "Well, this is why we pilot." Jane recalls this as a watershed moment in her career, one that permanently affected her attitude toward her leader and the organization, toward work, and toward responding to workplace issues. How do you suppose Jane felt? What was her perception about her new boss? What was Jane's perception about her future work? What did Jane learn about future interactions with that leader?

_____

_____

_____

_____

_____

_____

"Staying in touch" means just that. How often do you go to lunch, go for a jog, or spend half an hour over a cup of coffee with a constituent? Do you know what Jeff's particular work frustrations are? Do you know why Sahana is interested in working on an advanced degree part-time? How often do you ask people working in remote locations to join you for a "virtual lunch" via a web-conferencing product? What are some small things you could start doing to help you stay in touch?

_____

_____

_____

_____

_____

_____

_____

Ask Questions

Every question that you ask as a leader is a potential teaching opportunity, a moment of learning. Questions focus people's attention. The key to a good question is to think about the "quest" in your question: Where do you want to take this person with your question? What do you want this person to think about? Becoming more conscientious when asking questions forces you to understand what you are trying to teach and achieve. So consider carefully which two or three questions you want to ask about critical values and actions. Donna Goya, former vice president for human resources at Levi Strauss, explained that they never made "a key personnel decision without asking the question: 'Is this consistent with our aspirations?'"

What key questions should you always be asking of members of your organization or team? Why are these important?

_____

_____

_____

_____

_____

_____

If you are genuinely interested in what other people have to say, ask their opinion, especially before giving your own. Asking what others think facilitates participation in whatever decision will ultimately be determined. This subsequently increases support for the decision and reduces the risk that the decision might be undermined by either inadequate consideration or unexpected opposition. Another benefit is that asking others for their ideas and listening to their suggestions enhances their self-worth. People feel more important when they know that they can come to you with their ideas and be given a fair hearing—and that you consult with them and value their counsel before making decisions that may affect them.

Select two or three of the shared values in your organization, and then record two or three questions that would elicit responses about how people are acting on each value. For example, let's suppose one of the shared values is "innovation." You might ask: "What have you done in the last week to improve so that you are better this week than you were a week ago?" or "What have you changed lately?" or "What improvement have you tried recently that failed? What did you learn from that experience?" Refer back to the section in Chapter 5 where you listed your shared values, if necessary.

Shared Value 1: _____

Questions to ask:

_____

_____

_____

Shared Value 2: _____

Questions to ask:

_____

_____

_____

Shared Value 3: _____

Questions to ask:

_____

_____

_____

_____

Ask Better Questions

One of the complaints about traditional education is that "old school" teachers are always asking questions they already know the answer to, like, "What's 8 times 9?" "What's the capital of South Korea?" Students learn that memorizing the right things to say will earn them approval. They don't necessarily learn to think for themselves in this process.

Some better questions to ask focus on the big picture, the "why" behind a decision or action, and cause the listener to think about things in some new way. For example: "Can we figure out why this happened? We've done this for so long without a hitch. What was different today?" "What would happen if we did such-and-such? Have we tried looking at this from any other angle?"

And a great question that is timeless: "What do you think we can learn from this?"

Make Meaning, Daily

People make meaning of their situations by paying attention to the actions of their leaders, and especially to the congruence or disconnect between their leaders' words and their behaviors. To build and sustain credibility, you must give constituents positive and consistent images of how to act in ways that are consistent with shared values. Credible leaders understand and appreciate that people are always watching and paying attention to everything that they do.

Become a Storyteller

Storytelling is a major way that credible leaders teach others about what sense or meaning to make of various actions and achievements. Stories are powerful ways of getting your point across and bringing to life key values and norms about the way things are done in your organization. The key to being a good storyteller is to be authentic. Tell stories that have a personal connection for you.

In developing stories, think back on critical events: successes or missteps, times an employee made a startling discovery or the day someone went to extraordinary lengths to help a customer. Look for examples of times someone "walked the talk." Have a main character and a point of view in your story. Include relevant details, and build toward a climax or punch line.

Think of an important event in your company history or your own personal life. What was the story? Why did this event matter? What was the shared value illustrated or documented in this event?

_____

_____

_____

_____

_____

"How do we get people to act on our ideas? We tell stories."

—Chip Heath and Dan Heath, *Made to Stick*

Make Sure That Shared Values Are Being Talked About

The stories should usually not be about you! Create stories you can tell about what your constituents and peers are doing to put shared values into practice and to demonstrate their commitment as "disciples." Telling stories about others gives you the chance to reinforce the idea that everyone is a leader. Hearing or reading a story about people "like us" (people with whom we can identify) is also the most effective way to stimulate us to learn how to take such actions ourselves. Making people heroes encourages others to do the right thing. Besides, people seldom tire of hearing stories about themselves and people they know. Such stories tend to be repeated and the moral or lesson of the story is spread far and wide in the organization.

129

Where can you find stories? There is no shortage, once you appreciate where to look. Here are some of those places:

On Your Own: Set aside an hour each week for professional reading and research (if you aren't already actively doing that). Scan industry publications, websites, and blogs for examples of organizations, leaders, and constituents who are living the values they espouse.

On the Job: Make certain that everyone can champion the shared values. For example, at every staff meeting, randomly select someone to tell a story about how he or she "caught someone putting our values into practice." Everyone coming to the meeting will be aware that, through the luck of the draw, he or she may have the opportunity to share an occurrence that relates to shared values, and they'll be prepared week-after-week regardless of whether they are called upon in the meeting. Everyone will build up a repertoire of stories. These are stories that can be re-told by you and others long after that meeting is over.

Take this a step further and consider making storytelling the sole topic of your next meeting. Ask this question: "How is each of us putting our values into practice?" Be the first to describe what you have done. Even within very strong-culture organizations, the greatest challenges in maintaining people's focus and commitment have to do with ensuring that the actions and decisions of leaders are consistent with what they say and with what the institution recognizes and rewards.

Regain Lost Credibility

Credible leaders know what to do to regain credibility if they undermine, tarnish, or lose it. To build and sustain credibility, you must be able to execute the "Six A's of Leadership Accountability"—accept, admit, apologize, act, amend, and attend.

Think About a Time You . . .

Has there ever been a time when you felt you lost credibility with others? What were the circumstances, and what did you do?

_____

_____

_____

_____

_____

_____

What would you do differently next time?

_____

_____

_____

_____

_____

_____

To regain credibility, it's important that you apologize quickly and to the right people. You must tell the offended person that you are sincerely sorry.

(But you don't then have to go and tell the entire neighborhood that you are sorry.)

CBS Interactive commentator Eric Schurenberg, in a blog post on accountability, says, "Once you've taken blame, take ownership. Do something to show you are fixing the problem. A good example is Andersen's hiring of Paul Volcker to revamp their auditing practices. This action on their part lends credibility to the notion that the accounting firm is turning over a new leaf."[1]

Reduce Fear

As a leader, the better your interactions are with constituents, the easier it is for you to serve them—and to continue to serve them. Therefore, you need to be careful not to unintentionally create fear through your interactions with constituents. For example, certain abrasive and abusive conduct—such as obtrusive eye contact, silence, brevity or abruptness, snubbing or ignoring people, insults and put-downs, blaming, discrediting or discounting, aggressive mannerisms, job threats, yelling and shouting, angry outbursts, and physical threat—erect very thick walls of antagonism and resentment.[2] The effect is the same, by the way, whether these behaviors are intentional or not.

Making decisions behind closed doors (in secret) and failing to acknowledge or respond to people's input and suggestions also create tensions for people, primarily because of the ambiguity they create. Other enigmatic actions that contribute to making people afraid to interact with you include being inconsistent in your reasoning, acting cool and aloof or being impolite, playing favorites, claiming credit for someone else's ideas, communicating indirectly or through others, and being secretive.

You want to reduce these fear-producing behaviors and actions because the feelings they create work against the service relationship—in fact, they destroy it. All of them show a lack of caring, a lack of interest, and a lack of respect for the other person (your constituent). They assume that the "subordinate" is to serve the manager, rather than the customer. Eliminating these actions, some of which may admittedly be quite subtle, from your repertoire is essential to shifting from being the boss to being a servant leader. Open gestures, friendly looks, an inviting tone of voice, and being forthright and transparent all encourage others to trust you and become committed to shared values.

Think of a time someone who led you (or perhaps it was you) lost credibility. If you can't think of anyone, consider some famous fallen-from-grace public figures. What happened? Did they know what happened? Did they acknowledge it? Did they "own up" to it and apologize? If they tried to repair the damage, what did they do? Did it work? How long did it take to undo the damage done? What can you learn from this analysis?

Conclusion

What do you think people say about your leadership when you're not around? How do you feel about that? What would you have to do to change their opinions?

_____

_____

_____

_____

_____

_____

_____

Notes

1. Eric Schurenberg, http://marketplace.publicradio.org/features/archive_articles/commentary020224.htm. Used with his permission.
2. For more information, see K. Ryan & D. Oestreich, *Driving Fear Out of the Workplace* (2nd ed.). San Francisco: Jossey-Bass, 1998, p. 57.

CHAPTER EIGHT

Discipline 6:
Sustain Hope

Constituents want leaders with a positive, confident, can-do approach who remain passionate despite obstacles and setbacks. When leaders uplift spirits and restore people's belief in the future, they strengthen everyone's commitment and perseverance.

Start by thinking about the people or activities in your own environment that are uplifting your spirits and keeping your hope alive. What are they?

_____

_____

_____

What's missing for you? Reflecting on this might help to reveal some actions you need to take with others who might also be experiencing these gaps.

_____

_____

_____

Now, what are some of the specific ways your leadership keeps hope alive? What everyday actions do you take to enable constituents to believe in their capacity to overcome difficulties and reach challenging goals? What do you do to encourage positivity, open people to new possibilities, and breed optimism? What needs to change?

_____

_____

_____

_____

_____

_____

_____

Write Your Vision of the Future

Positive and unique mental images of the future are also necessary for sustaining hope. People can only have hope if they can see a better future ahead. Additionally, constituents expect their leaders to be forward-looking. Leaders must have a sense of direction and a positive ideal image of the future for the common good. The ability to imagine and enlist others in a compelling vision of the future distinguishes credible leaders from other credible individuals.

Being optimistic and hopeful means finding the future by staring out into the unknown and imagining the possibilities. It means visualizing the future in some detail. It means being creative about options. To increase your credibility, this vision needs to incorporate and encompass the aspirations of your constituents so that your vision of the future is shared by everyone. You can think about the future all by yourself, but eventually this has to become a dialogue, not a monologue. Leaders engage in dialogues with constituents about what they see across the horizon of time, seeking a common vision that all can share.

One place to start is by asking yourself this question: "Are we in this job to do something, or are we in this job for something to do?" Your answer will most likely be: "To do something" Assuming this is the case, then take out a piece of paper and at the top write: "What we want to accomplish." Write down a list of items to be accomplished. Then consider each entry and ask yourself: "Why do we want this?" Keep asking "why" at least five times in order to increase your depth of understanding. By doing this exercise, you are likely to discover a few higher-order, long-term values that are idealized ends for which you strive. An example is provided below. Following that is some space for you to reflect deeply on your own goals, which can be used in preparation for doing this exercise with your team.

What We Want to Accomplish

Example: We want to develop and launch a new product.

Why? Because it will fill a key hole in our product offerings to customers.
Why? Because it will improve our profit margins.
Why? Because it will enhance the reputation and importance of this work group.
Why? Because we say we are all about solving customer problems through innovation.
Why? Because this will prove that we can be responsive and creative.

Why? Because this will be an enormously exciting, challenging, and
rewarding opportunity that will test and stretch our competencies.

Why? Because we have the chance to improve the way people live and work.

Why? Because we can contribute to a more sustainable planet.

1. _____

   Why? _____

   _____

   _____

   _____

   Why? _____

   _____

   _____

   _____

   Why? _____

   _____

   _____

   _____

   Why? _____

   _____

   _____

   _____

   Why? _____

_____

_____

_____

2. _____

Why? _____

_____

_____

_____

Why? _____

_____

_____

_____

Why? _____

_____

_____

_____

Why? _____

_____

_____

_____

Why? _____

_____

_____

_____

Now that you've taken some time to think about why you do what you do, you can see how this might translate into a vision statement. What is the ideal and unique image of the future for the common good in terms of your work, your constituents, and your organization?

_____

_____

_____

_____

_____

_____

_____

Be careful when working to articulate your vision to understand the options available, and use your imagination. Henry Ford once said if he'd asked the public what they wanted, the public would have said "A faster horse." Don't just imagine polishing what's already there. What, in your wildest dreams, do you really want to see happen?

Set Goals and Make a Plan

Hopeful and optimistic people have more than positive images of the future; they have goals and plans for how they will achieve them. Take your vision statement, break it down into projects, set goals for each, and make a plan to achieve them. And should you find that you are not meeting your plan, don't frustrate yourself and your group. Be flexible and change the plan or re-set your targets.

The best goals are SMART: specific, measurable, attainable, results-oriented, and time-bound. Use these criteria when making your plans. What exact outcomes will you accomplish? How will you know when you reach them? How will you measure your success? How will you know whether the goals are within your reach and the group's reach? By when will you have accomplished them?

Example: *My goal is to start having dinner with my family every night. This will involve managing my calendar so I am out of here by 6 p.m. Rather than stay here working late, I'll identify some tasks each day I can do at home after dinner, rather than do them at the office. Success will be making it home for dinner at least four nights each week. Next week I'll try for two nights, then three the following week, then make it to four by the end of the month and maintain that.*

Goal 1. What will your success look like? By when?

_____

_____

_____

_____

_____

_____

_____

_____

Take another tip from the optimists and plan small wins.[1] Awesome challenges and wrenching changes can overwhelm people. Major social and economic problems can seem impossible to solve. Leaders know that the most effective change strategies are processes of accumulating little incremental victories—even when the ultimate goal is a complete overhaul of the system. The ultimate goal should be a stretch. But as you plan for that goal, set incremental objectives that are easily achievable. To sustain hope, divide tasks into small chunks, reduce tasks to their bare essentials, make things doable in brief time periods, experiment continuously, and move forward with the natural innovation adoption cycle.

Take Charge

In keeping hope alive, credible leaders demonstrate their faith and confidence by first accepting responsibility for the quality of their lives as well as for the lives of their constituents. They take charge. They recognize that, although they cannot control 100 percent of what goes on in life, it is possible to exert internal control, rather than being controlled externally by others or events.

A critical aspect of taking charge is being proactive. This means owning the situation or problem before it owns you, or forestalling it completely.

Proactivity begins when you believe that you can be a force for positive change—and when you are prepared to put a lot of effort and hard work into overcoming obstacles that get in your way. So test your readiness to take charge by answering a few questions. When answering these questions, keep in mind the vision and goals that you wrote about in the opening exercise:

1. How convinced are you that you can be a powerful force for positive change when working toward your vision? Circle the number on the scale below that best represents where you see yourself.

1	2	3	4	5	6	7
No influence						In charge

2. How ready are you to deal with the inevitable obstacles that you will encounter along the way?

1	2	3	4	5	6	7
Unprepared						Completely prepared

3. How much do you enjoy working on difficult challenges?

1	2	3	4	5	6	7
Avoid them						Love them

4. When you encounter setbacks in your work, what do you do?

1	2	3	4	5	6	7
Give up						Never give up

What does this simple assessment tell you about your sense of your own power and influence, your readiness to take on challenges, your energy and passion for change, and your persistence?

_____

_____

_____

_____

_____

What are some things you can do to make sure you enhance your ability to take charge of change?

_____

_____

_____

Focus on the Future

Another great way to be proactive is to work ahead. Stay on top of trends, make time for professional reading, take a class, and pay attention to what those around you are talking about. It's important to see the future and be ready for it. What are some future trends you are most excited about?

_____

_____

_____

Focus on Proactive Phrases

Reactive people are driven by feelings, circumstances, conditions, and other people. They react to things around them; often, they let the things around them control them. They seem to be victims of their own circumstances and fail to see that they have choices or opportunities to exercise their personal power. ***Proactive* people are driven by values**—the things they say have meaning for them and are worthy of their commitment, and they make choices accordingly. Credible leaders are proactive: they know who they are, what they want to do, and why. They reflect this in how they react to things that happen around them, and they set an example for others in how to frame their experiences in proactive (take charge) ways through the ways they verbalize their reactions to life's events and interruptions. Proactivity also leads to a more optimistic outlook on life.

End-of-Day Activity

At the end of one of your work days, stop and think back. How many times did you use reactive language? Consider your use of phrases like "I can't," "I have to," and "if only."

_____

_____

Proactive leaders use proactive language. Circle the language below that you think you need to start using or need to use more:

"Let's look at some alternatives."

"I want to. . . ."

"I choose to. . . ."

"I will. . . ."

"I would rather. . . ."

"I can make the time."

"I need to prioritize my obligations."

145

As a leader, it's also important for you to keep a finger on the pulse of your constituents being reactive and proactive. Pay attention to how often you hear reactive phrases from them. Are employees always saying they aren't *allowed* to do this or that? Do you hear them tell customers that they *can't* accommodate a request or fix a problem? Is that true? Do they get in trouble for bending rules or achieving unusual solutions? If so, it is your job to help untie their hands.

What do you need to do to help constituents move toward more proactive mindsets? Helping them to reframe their reactive language to more proactive behavior may often require substantive changes—more than simply instituting a positive spin. For example, do they need more help understanding available actions? Are they not clear about their choices? Do they feel you won't support them if they take a risk?

_____

_____

_____

_____

_____

_____

_____

Choose Optimism Appropriately

Credible leaders are optimistic—they have a positive, uplifting outlook on life. They don't deny the facts nor are they unrealistic about the challenges and possible hardships that lie ahead. They also listen to the pessimists around them because their views may also provide invaluable information and insight. So, while choosing to be optimistic and hopeful, do so appropriately. Here are several guidelines that can be useful for you in selecting optimism[2]:

- If you are in an achievement situation (receiving a promotion, selling a product, writing a difficult report, winning a game), use optimism.
- If you are concerned about how you will feel (fighting off depression, keeping up morale), use optimism.
- If the situation is apt to be protracted and your physical health is an issue, use optimism.
- If you want to lead, if you want to inspire others, if you want people to vote for you, use optimism.
- If your goal is to counsel others whose future is dim, do not use optimism initially.
- If you want to appear sympathetic to the troubles of others, do not begin with optimism, although using it later, once confidence and empathy are established, may help.
- If your goal is to plan for a risky and uncertain future, do not use optimism.

This is not to say, however, that you should necessarily choose pessimism in any of these circumstances. The point is to temper your approach from unfettered to flexible optimism.

Make an "Enough" List

Work with your constituents to develop an "enough" list. Ask for input in a meeting or provide a box for anonymous comments. Ask each person to name one thing about him- or herself, the office, the work, the building, each other, that does not need to change—something there is enough of and they are content with. Some answers might be:

- "We get enough done."
- "I have enough leeway to do my job as I see fit."
- "I have enough support from my co-workers."
- "I have enough face time with my manager."
- "I have enough access to resources I need."

Post these on a poster, or revisit a few at the start of staff meetings. It won't eliminate talk of "what we don't have enough of," but it will help to put people in a positive, solution-focused frame of mind. Being positive stretches people's minds, opens them up to new possibilities, and expands their worldviews.

Arouse Positive Thoughts and Images

Being supportive is how leaders sustain hope over time. Listening to constituents, developing and helping others, increasing others' self-esteem, and expressing genuine concern and caring are all behaviors of credible leaders. This form of encouragement is something that you can do in business (and in your personal life) every day.

In staying positive, it is important for you to manifest, and model, adaptability and resilience. It is also important that you view "defeats" (mistakes and setbacks) as temporary and having specific, rather than universal, causes. Ask yourself: "Are the images I paint of the future positive or negative ones?" "When the going gets tough, do I join in the struggle or let others go it alone?"

_____

_____

_____

Think about the last several work weeks. When things go wrong, do you bounce back by taking charge of the situation or stand idly by? When a failure or setback occurs, do you blame yourself or blame others? Do you see it as a permanent situation or a temporary one that you can do something about? And when something good happens, do you see this as connected to your own actions rather than luck or circumstances? What could you do differently to increase your capacity to sustain hope and be more optimistic? What can you do to help others to do the same?

_____

_____

_____

_____

_____

_____

Dispute Negative Beliefs

In order to become more optimistic, you have to learn to dispute any negative explanations about the bad things that happen. Professor Martin Seligman offers the ABCDE model (adversity, belief, consequences, disputation, and energization) as one very effective technique for doing this. As he explains: "When we encounter adversity, we react by thinking about it. Our thoughts rapidly congeal into beliefs. These beliefs may become so habitual we don't even stop and focus on them. And they don't just sit there idly; they have consequences."[3] If, when you encounter adversity, you tend to explain it in the form of personal, permanent, and pervasive factors, you are likely to give up and become paralyzed. If, however, you view adversity as a temporary hurdle, you become energized.

How do you move from the consequences of your beliefs to energy? The first step in becoming more optimistic is reflective: record specific adversities, your beliefs about them, and the consequences of your beliefs. Identify those adverse circumstances that you explain with negative, disturbing beliefs. Now, dispute the negative beliefs. Find an optimistic explanation for adversity—an explanation that will make you positive about the future and cause you to feel less overwhelmed, more relaxed, and better about yourself. Successfully dispute beliefs and you'll be energized. One example is provided below; following is room for you to record and then examine one from your own experience.

Example: *You are running late for work. Another driver swerves into your lane without signaling, causing you to slam on the brakes. The other driver then zooms ahead and swerves back into another lane. You yell, "Jerk!" as you feel your blood pressure rise. You arrive at work in a grouchy mood.*

Initial explanation: *Other people are so inconsiderate. That guy ruined my morning.*

Disputations: *Wow, he must have a really bad life to need to take out his frustrations by driving like that. Or, I remember doing that the day my son broke his arm and I was trying to rush him to the hospital as quickly as possible and that's all I was thinking about. Perhaps he's dealing with a similar situation. I'm going to back off and give him all the room he needs.*

150

My example:

_____

_____

_____

_____

Initial explanation:

_____

_____

_____

_____

Disputations:

_____

_____

_____

_____

_____

_____

Try this same technique with your group. Look for explanations that will evoke positive energy in the group and consequently spur everyone on to higher levels of achievement.

Look for the Silver Lining

Here's an activity you can do on your own or with your constituents in a group setting. When dealing with an adverse event—a misstep, a mistake, a loss, a setback—work to find the silver lining. For example:

1. "We lost that sale, but we built a good relationship with the client and are hopeful for future business with them."
2. "I had trouble with that presentation, but the group responded really well to the statistics we presented regarding the user base."
3. "That didn't go as well as we hoped, but something we can fix in the future is. . . ."

Use the space provided in the "silver lining" clouds to write your own statements.

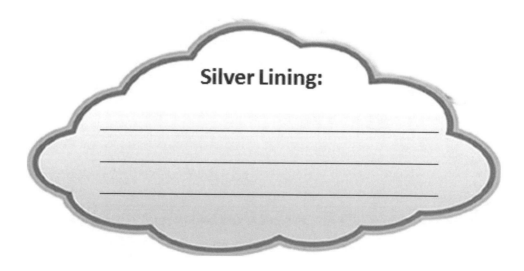

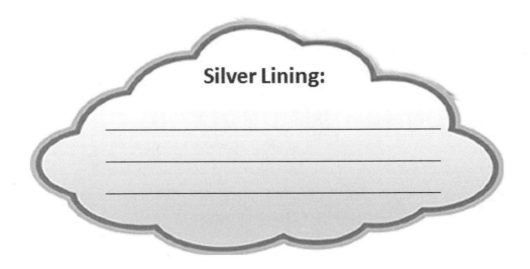

Unleash Passion

As a leader it's vital that you find, employ, and display your own passion. What ignites your best energy and thinking? Thinking up a new marketing plan, working on researching a new product, seeing assembly completed? You need to pay attention, too, to the "passion level" of those you lead. Many people start out in their jobs energized and passionate. But time and stresses and demands can lead to burnout and decreased passion.

Work through the questions below. Give short answers, but examine the topic in as much depth as possible. Try to think of these as conversation starters. Discuss them with others, and ask others to share their own thoughts. Could you answer these questions about your constituents?

What do you most love to do?

_____

_____

_____

What are some things you would love to be able to do with your life?

_____

_____

_____

What are the most important things in your life at this time?

_____

_____

_____

What special talents, personality characteristics, or abilities do you possess?

_____

_____

_____

List three of your favorite things to do in your spare time:

1. _____

2. _____

3. _____

What about each of these things brings you joy?

_____

_____

_____

Do they have anything in common?

_____

_____

_____

If you could go back and change one direction your life has taken, what would you change?

_____

_____

_____

When your life is over, what would you like people to say about you?

_____

_____

_____

What do you think is your purpose in life?

_____

_____

_____

Do you feel that purpose as a burning desire inside of you?

_____

_____

_____

Does your purpose keep you interested and energized, even when others give up or burn out?

_____

_____

_____

Would you pursue your passion, even if you were not paid to do so?

_____

_____

_____

By achieving your purpose, would you instill passion in other people?

_____

_____

_____

Would other people come to you to find out what your "secret" is?

_____

_____

_____

What is your organizational mission?

_____

_____

_____

What is your departmental mission/goals?

_____

_____

_____

What is your personal purpose/goals?

_____

_____

_____

What personal goals do you have in common with your organization or department?

_____

_____

_____

Where are your own goals not in congruence with those of your workplace?

_____

_____

_____

What steps could you take to realign your personal goals with those of the workplace?*

_____

_____

_____

*Questions are from Patricia Boverie and Michael Kroth, "Passion and Purpose." *The 2001 Annual: Volume 1, Training.* San Francisco: Pfeiffer. Reprinted with permission of John Wiley & Sons, Inc.

The activity above asked you to consider your own level of passion. But your being passionate is only half the equation. What are you doing to ignite passion in others? Do they share your passion?

Give Love and Support

The leader who shows love through enthusiasm for the work, who expresses concern for constituents, and who invests in helping to create a caring workplace, will find an easier path in drawing others to common goals and activities. People want to be included in such a situation. And people who feel loved and supported are naturally more hopeful.

Some strategies for giving love and support are listed below. For each, think also about how the activities tie to the values you've explored throughout this workbook.

Personalize Recognition

Where one constituent might put great stock in positive comments on an annual performance review, another might prefer lunch out with the leader. Where one might value an award bestowed during a public event, another might be embarrassed and prefer a quiet "thank you." Where one customer values a 10 percent one-time discount, another might prefer a personal check-in call every quarter. Recognition needs to be meaningful; making it meaningful requires you to get to know constituents as individuals. Think about three constituents or constituent groups, and imagine they have done something you wish to reward (or, if a customer, want to thank them for). What might be especially meaningful to each?

159   ·

Constituent 1: _____

_____

_____

Constituent 2: _____

_____

_____

Constituent 3: _____

_____

_____

_____

- Remember birthdays. Pay attention to news of children's graduations, the birth of a child or grandchild, or the loss of a parent. Say something when you hear that news.
- Demonstrate love and giving through community involvement or charity work. Make it known that constituents are welcome, but not compelled, to join in.
- Do something visible and voluntary that makes the world a little better for constituents. A coat of paint, a better chair, or the smell of warm cookies on Friday afternoons can do wonders for feelings of goodwill.
- Ask a constituent to teach you something, based on his or her expertise. This could be work-related but also could be a guitar lesson, an overview

of the art of scrapbooking, a class in making sushi, or an hour spent together rearranging your office according to the principles of Feng Shui.

- "Treasure Box." In a public area shared by constituents, put out a "treasure box"—anything with a closed lid—and a supply of index cards or a notepad. Several times per month, remind employees to write down something good that has happened, from the air conditioning being repaired to a big sale to a compliment from a customer to an exceptionally good entrée in the company cafeteria. Keep the cards in the treasure box. Occasionally, during a meeting or other gathering, pull a few items out of the box and read them aloud. Use this as a starting point for a short general discussion of things that are going well and a reminder to look for positives and set an expectation of continued future accomplishments.

Nurture Optimism and Hope Through Interactions

One way to offer support is by increasing your personal interactions with others. Another positive by-product is that, by listening to other people (indicating that you find them and their ideas worth your time!) and getting to know them, you enhance their trust in you. So make a simple commitment to start your day by chatting with your constituents. Stop by your colleagues' offices or cubicles, or even send an e-mail or text message and ask how they are doing. Ask what someone did last night, or what good news he or she might have to share or what problems you might be able to help with. With each person, find out something you didn't know before. Be self-disclosing yourself and let others know about the things that bring joy to your life, as this also enhances trust and credibility.

161

Let's say you have fifty constituents. That's ten to visit each work day to see everyone each week. At five minutes with each, that's less than one hour per day. If strengthening credibility is the goal, there is no more productive way to spend that hour than talking one-on-one with your constituents. When people believe that someone understands them and has their best interests at heart, they give that person more credibility. Assuming, of course, you do it with good cheer. If you wake up on the wrong side of the bed and feel grumpy, you're likely to make others feel grumpy, too. Emotions are contagious. Literally. Moods are social viruses, and you can catch a bad mood as easily as a bad cold. You can also catch a good mood.[4] So make a conscious effort to infect others with your good mood. How would you go about started this?

_____

_____

_____

Leaders know that in supporting their constituents they need to attend to work/life balance issues. But the idea of work/life balance means more than just carving out ample time for family and job; it means giving thought to and nurturing the whole person. Constituents who give the leader their energy and commitment can become drained. Encourage your constituents to remember to "fill their cups." Tell them that giving is wonderful, but their cups will run dry if they never replenish them. Career satisfaction can be supported by an occasional "mental health day," educational opportunities, time for community service projects, and time for professional self-renewal.

Remember, hope is an attitude in action. With hope, optimism, and a positive attitude, credible leaders make it possible for themselves and others to achieve more than they originally thought possible. Being possibility-thinkers enables people to transcend the difficulties of today in favor of a better tomorrow. They bounce back more resiliently from setbacks, persevering and making the sacrifices often necessary to do things that have never been done before. With support, encouragement, optimism, and a positive hopeful outlook, we find the will and the way to greatness.

Notes

1. See J. M. Kouzes & B. Z. Posner (2007). *The Leadership Challenge*, pp. 217–238. See also Goleman, in Note 4 below.
2. Seligman, M. E. (1990). *Learned Optimism.* New York: Alfred A. Knopf, pp. 208–209.
3. Seligman, op. cit., p. 211. The ABCDE model is based on the work of pioneering psychologist Albert Ellis. For a complete description of the model, see pages 208–280.
4. Goleman, D. (1991, October 15). "Happy, or Sad, a Mood Can Prove Contagious." *The New York Times*, p. B5.

CHAPTER NINE

The Struggle to
Be Human

Sustaining credibility is one of the most perplexing leadership conundrums of our times. How can anyone speak with certainty about an uncertain, turbulent future? How can consensus be achieved when the choices are vast and the speed of decision making and the consequences of making them are so quick? How can a leader remain consistent when the situation keeps changing?

This isn't the first time leaders have had to puzzle over such confusing conditions. Recall these words of Charles Dickens from *A Tale of Two Cities,* published in 1859:

> "It was the best of times, it was the worst of times, it was the age of wisdom, it was the age of foolishness, it was the epoch of belief, it was the epoch of incredulity, it was the season of Light, it was the season of Darkness, it was the spring of hope, it was the winter of despair, we had everything before us, we had nothing before us, we were all going direct to heaven, we were all going direct the other way."

There have never been any easy answers to difficult questions. Leaders always have to wrestle with ambiguity, uncertainty, and change. But of this you can be certain: Credibility is the foundation of leadership. Act in ways that increase people's belief that you are honest, competent, inspiring, and forward-looking, and people will be much more likely to want to follow your direction.

Tensions a Leader Must Face

To earn and sustain credibility, you must experience and act upon the tensions that characterize organizational life today—the tension between freedom and constraint, the tension between leading and following, and the tension over what defines success. In your experience, how strong is each of these tensions? Rate them using the following scale:

1 = Not very strong   3 = Moderately strong   5 = Very strong

1. The tension between freedom and constraint 1   2   3   4   5

2. The tension between leading and following   1   2   3   4   5

3. The tension over what defines success   1   2   3   4   5

Tension Between Freedom and Constraint

As a leader, when have you encountered tensions between freedom and constraint? What did you do?

_____

_____

_____

What was the outcome? How did it look through the eyes of your constituents? Would you do anything differently next time? If so, what?

———————————————————————

———————————————————————

———————————————————————

Tension Between Leading and Following

When have you felt at odds with the leaders above you? Have you ever felt a conflict in deciding when to lead and when to follow?

———————————————————————

———————————————————————

———————————————————————

———————————————————————

The research about what people look for in their leaders reveals that people want their *leaders* to be forward-looking and inspiring. However, when asked about what they look for in their colleagues, this is not what they want. What they want from colleagues is *dependability* and *cooperativeness,* and these are sometimes at odds with being forward-looking. Have you ever felt pressured to just go along rather than continue to push your own agenda and values? What was the experience like? What did you do?

———————————————————————

———————————————————————

———————————————————————

———————————————————————

What can you do to encourage and tolerate the internal conflict necessary to reconcile this? Both for yourself and when observing this being played out among your co-workers and direct reports? Putting people in charge of their own decision making—developing the leader in everyone—will require relaxing expectations of abiding devotion.

_____

_____

_____

_____

Tension Over What Defines Success

What is your idea of "success" in terms of being a credible leader? Is it changing the world or changing the 2,500 square feet of office space for which you're responsible? Choose a future date, two years or five years or ten years from now, and imagine you are leaving this role for another—perhaps for another job in the same organization or for a job elsewhere. What are some things that will tell you that you succeeded? What will give you satisfaction about what you are leaving behind? What do you need to do now to ensure you reach this goal? List your "success markers" here:

1. _____

_____

_____

_____

2. _____

_____

_____

_____

_____

3. _____

_____

_____

_____

From Excellence to Excess

The "Six Disciplines of Credibility" are a means for building the foundation of leadership. However, excessive focus on a discipline for the sake of perfecting the method instead of producing the intended result is triumph of technique over purpose; for each extreme effect, however, there is an antidote. Too much of a good thing can be, well, too much. No one wants a leader who turns into a rabid evangelist or the equivalent of a motivational huckster. There's a fine line between confidence and egomania. The Six Disciplines of Credibility are guidelines for growth, something to strive for. Taken to extremes, you can cross the line to behaviors that undermine the very credibility you're trying to build. Let's look at each of these challenges and its antidote.

From Self-Discovery to Arrogance

Becoming too self-aware, too sure of one's own abilities, can lead to the perception that one is an over-confident know-it-all. **Antidote: Practice openness**.

Some time in the next week, create an opportunity to learn something from someone else, ask for and listen—really listen—to someone's point of view on an issue about which you have strong feelings, or watch for a chance to say, "I was wrong about that" or "I'm open to rethinking that." Document the experience here:

_____

_____

_____

_____

_____

_____

_____

From Appreciation to Fragmentation

It is important to value differences and diversity, to encourage debate and to challenge old ways of thinking. But it isn't possible to please all of the people all of the time. Too much emphasis on appreciating difference puts the leader at risk. **Antidote: Complexity**

When standing close to a problem, it is easy to view it through a simple, small frame. But human relationships and interactions are anything but simple.

As a leader, remember to step back and take a 50,000-foot, 360-degree view of situations and try to understand the view from several different points of view. Step back for a moment and think of a time you felt fragmentation. Who were the different people or what fragments were involved? What was the point of view of each? How can this inform your actions next time?

_____

_____

_____

_____

_____

_____

_____

From Affirmation to Rigidity

Too much consensus and sharing of group values can lead to groupthink. It's important to lead with shared values, but without starting a cult. **Antidote: Challenge**

Look for opportunities to challenge thinking, to play devil's advocate, to ask people why they have a particular value, why they believe in it, whether it is still useful. Intentionally introduce some conversation around this topic at the next gathering of constituents. Document the experience here:

_____

_____

_____

_____

_____

_____

_____

_____

From Development to Vanity

Learning, and mastery, is about the journey, not about achieving perfection. Perfection leads to continual dissatisfaction: the world will never be "perfect." Never. And the leader looking for perfection from constituents will never be satisfied and will never let constituents do things their own way. **Antidote: Humility**

Just as the credible leader celebrates successes, so will that leader bring mistakes out into the open. Debrief them and examine them. Don't spend time on blame, but instead ask, "What can we learn from this?" If you are responsible for the error, then acknowledge it, apologize, and make it right. Be on the lookout for an opportunity to explore and work through a mistake with constituents, in the spirit of learning, not worrying. Document your experience here:

_____

_____

_____

_____

_____

_____

_____

From Serving to Subservience

The credible leader must listen, but at some point the listening must lead to a decision, to action, to follow through. It is a challenge to decide when to respond to constituents and when to act on your own. You are, after all, the leader, and the leader is always in danger of losing him- or herself to the cause, to become subsumed by the work and those in the workplace. **Antidote: Independence**

Work is important, but not when it is the only thing you have. A passion for one's work is vital to the credibility of a leader, but it's crucial that you have interests and an identity beyond the scope of your work. Outside interests are also critical to supporting your objectivity, your ability to stand outside the work you do and to view it with a critical eye.

Other than your role as a leader, how do you identify yourself? What are some areas of interest or pursuits outside of your organization? Are they enough?

_____

_____

_____

_____

Where would you like to develop additional interests? What skills do you possess that you can apply to other areas?

_____

_____

_____

_____

_____

From Sustaining to Dependence

It is important to support constituents, to accommodate their varied needs and help them achieve a reasonable balance between work and their private lives. But too much support can foster dependency. Letting others lead, or at least giving them freedom to act, helps them become more self-reliant and self-directed, and this ultimately makes *your* job easier.

Antidote: Action

For the next few weeks, watch for opportunities to encourage people to act, to make decisions, or to make a difference. Watch out for talk that suggests people are helpless or that their contributions don't matter, and take steps to recognize and reward exceptional performance. Document your experience here:

_____

_____

_____

_____

_____

_____

_____

_____

_____

Initiate Renewal: New Beginnings from the Old Ending

Eventually, energy burns down, ideas become stale, and initiatives seem passé. Be alert to the possibility of getting stuck, of recognizing when old behaviors and plans are no longer working. Remember, the credible leader focuses on the journey, not the destination. You should never stop learning and growing and changing. One of the most-admired traits of the leader is that he or she is forward-looking—so keep looking ahead. Ask yourself, "In the next six months, what will I do to be building and renewing my leadership credibility?"

_____

_____

_____

_____

_____

And in another six months, ask yourself that question again.

175

Now—right now—put the question on your calendar for six months from today, and every six months thereafter, so you will remember to ask it again—and again. Remember that the end of every adventure is simply the start of a new one!

Characteristics of an Admired Leader

- ☐ Ambitious (aspiring, hardworking, striving)
- ☐ Broad-Minded (open-minded, flexible, receptive, tolerant)
- ☐ Caring (appreciative, compassionate, concerned, loving, nurturing)
- ☐ Competent (capable, proficient, effective, gets the job done, professional)
- ☐ Cooperative (collaborative, team player, responsive)
- ☐ Courageous (bold, daring, risk-taker, gutsy)
- ☐ Dependable (reliable, conscientious, responsible)
- ☐ Determined (dedicated, resolute, persistent, purposeful)
- ☐ Fair-Minded (just, unprejudiced, objective, forgiving, willing to pardon others)
- ☐ Forward-Looking (visionary, foresighted, future-oriented, has direction)

- ☐ Honest (truthful, has integrity, trustworthy, has character, is trusting)
- ☐ Imaginative (creative, innovative, curious)
- ☐ Independent (self-reliant, self-sufficient, self-confident)
- ☐ Inspiring (uplifting, enthusiastic, energetic, humorous, cheerful, optimistic, positive about future)
- ☐ Intelligent (bright, smart, thoughtful, intellectual, reflective, logical)
- ☐ Loyal (faithful, dutiful, unswerving in allegiance, devoted)
- ☐ Mature (experienced, wise, has depth)
- ☐ Self-Controlled (restrained, self-disciplined)
- ☐ Straightforward (direct, candid, forthright)
- ☐ Supportive (helpful, offers assistance, comforting)

ABOUT THE AUTHORS

Jim Kouzes and Barry Posner are co-authors of the award-winning and international best-selling book, *The Leadership Challenge.* This book was selected as one of the top ten books on leadership of all time (according to *The 100 Best Business Books of All Time*), won the James A. Hamilton Hospital Administrators' Book-of-the-Year Award and the Critics' Choice Award from the nation's book review editors, was a *Business Week* best-seller, and has sold nearly two million copies in more than twenty languages. Jim and Barry have co-authored more than a dozen other leadership books, including *The Truth About Leadership, A Leader's Legacy*—selected by *Soundview Executive Book Summaries* as one of the top thirty books of the year—*Credibility: How Leaders Gain It and Lose It, Why People Demand It*—chosen by *Industry Week* as one of its year's five best management books—*Encouraging the Heart, The Student Leadership Challenge,* and *The Academic Administrator's Guide to Exemplary Leadership.* They also developed the highly acclaimed *Leadership Practices Inventory* (LPI), a 360-degree questionnaire for assessing leadership behavior, which is one of the most widely used leadership assessment instruments in the world. More than five hundred doctoral dissertations and academic research projects have been based on the Five Practices of Exemplary Leadership® model.

Among the honors and awards that Jim and Barry have received are the American Society for Training and Development's (ASTD) highest award for their Distinguished Contribution to Workplace Learning and Performance; Management/Leadership Educators of the Year by the International Management Council (this honor puts them in the company of Ken Blanchard, Stephen Covey, Peter Drucker, Edward Deming, Frances Hesselbein, Lee Iacocca, Rosabeth Moss Kanter, Norman Vincent Peale, and Tom Peters, who are all past recipients of the award); and named among the Top 50 Leadership Coaches in the nation (according to *Coaching for Leadership*).

Jim and Barry are frequent conference speakers, and each has conducted leadership development programs for hundreds of organizations, including Apple, Applied Materials, ARCO, AT&T, Australia Post, Bank of America, Bose, Charles Schwab, Chevron, Cisco Systems, Community Leadership Association, Conference Board of Canada, Consumers Energy, Dell Computer, Deloitte Touche, Dorothy Wylie Nursing Leadership Institute, Dow Chemical, Egon Zehnder International, FedEx, Genetech, Gymboree, HP, IBM, Intel, Jobs DR-Singapore, Johnson & Johnson, Kaiser Foundation Health Plans and Hospitals, L. L. Bean, Lawrence Livermore National Labs, Lucile Packard Children's Hospital, Merck, Motorola, NetApp, Northrop Grumman, Oakwood Temporary Housing, Roche, Siemens, 3M, Toyota, United Way, USAA, Verizon, VISA, and The Walt Disney Company. They have also lectured and made presentation on over fifty college campus around the world.

Jim Kouzes is a professional speaker and executive coach, and *The Wall Street Journal* has cited him as one of the twelve best executive educators in the

United States. In 2006 Jim was presented with the Golden Gavel, the highest honor awarded by Toastmasters International. Jim served as president, CEO, and chairman of the Tom Peters Company from 1988 through 1999, and prior to that led the Executive Development Center at Santa Clara University (1981–1987). Jim founded the Joint Center for Human Services Development at San Jose State University (1972–1980) and was on the staff of the School of Social Work, University of Texas. His career in training and development began in 1969 when he conducted seminars for Community Action Agency staff and volunteers in the war on poverty effort. Following graduation from Michigan State University (B.A. with honors in political science), he served as a Peace Corps volunteer (1967–1969). Jim also received a certificate from San Jose State University's School of Business for completion of the internship in organization development. Jim can be reached at jim@kouzes.com.

Barry Posner is professor of leadership at Santa Clara University (Silicon Valley, California), where he has received numerous teaching and innovation awards and served as dean of the Leavey School of Business for twelve years (1997–2009). An internationally renowned scholar and educator, Barry is author or co-author of more than a hundred research and practitioner-focused articles. He currently serves on the editorial review boards for *Leadership and Organizational Development, Leadership Review,* and *The International Journal of Servant-Leadership.* Barry is a warm and engaging conference speaker and dynamic workshop facilitator. Barry received his baccalaureate degree with honors from the University of California, Santa Barbara, in political science; his master's degree from The Ohio State University in public administration; and his doctoral degree from the University of Massachusetts, Amherst, in organizational behavior and administrative theory. Having consulted with a wide variety of public and private sector organizations around the globe, Barry currently sits on the board of directors of EMQ FamiliesFirst. He has served previously on the boards of Advanced Energy Industries (NASDAQ), American Institute of Architects (AIA), Big Brothers/Big Sisters of Santa Clara County, Center for Excellence in Nonprofits, Junior Achievement of Silicon Valley and Monterey Bay, Public Allies, San Jose Repertory Theater, Sigma Phi Epsilon Fraternity, and several start-up companies. Barry can be reached at bposner@scu.edu.

Jane Bozarth is an internationally known trainer, speaker, and author. A training practitioner since 1989, Jane is a graduate of the University of North Carolina at Chapel Hill, has an M.Ed. in training and development/ technology in training from North Carolina State University, and completed her doctorate in training and development in 2008. She is the author of Pfeiffer's *e-Learning Solutions on a Shoestring; Better Than Bullet Points: Creating Engaging e-Learning with PowerPoint; From Analysis to Evaluation,* and, with Jim Kouzes and Barry Posner, *The Challenge Continues.* In addition to her work as e-learning coordinator for the state of North Carolina, Jane has a longstanding collaborative relationship with InSync Training, LLC, and serves as their social media strategist.

Jane is the recipient of a Live and Online Award, a *Training* magazine Editor's Pick Award, and a North Carolina State University Distinguished Alumni Award for Outstanding Contributions to Practice.

Jane and her husband, Kent Underwood, live in Durham, North Carolina. She can be contacted via her website www.bozarthzone.com, via Facebook at Jane Bozarth Bozarthzone, and via Twitter at @janebozarth.

More Products from Kouzes and Posner

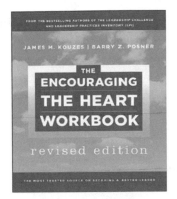

ISBN: 978-0-470-87683-1
US $19.95/CAN $23.95

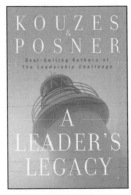

ISBN: 978-0-470-47918-6
US $18.95/CAN $20.95

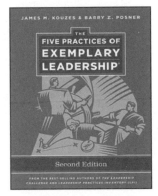

ISBN: 978-0-470-90734-4
US $10.00   /CAN $11.00

Getting extraordinary things done in organizations is hard work. To maintain the sparks of hope and determination, you as a leader must be able to motivate your team with appreciation, courage, and hope.

In this provocative book, Jim Kouzes and Barry Posner explore the question of leadership and legacy. In twenty-two chapters, they examine the questions all leaders must ask themselves in order to leave a lasting impact.

This 16-page article is perfect for leaders with limited time and budget. It provides a concise overview of Kouzes and Posner's model and overall thoughts on leadership.

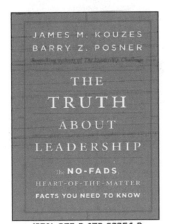

ISBN: 978-0-470-63354-0
US $24.95/CAN $29.95

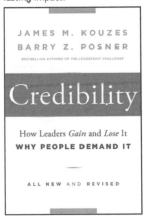

ISBN: 978-0-470-65171-1
US $27.95/CAN $33.95

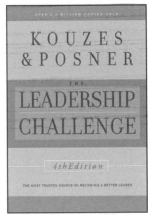

ISBN: 978-0-7879-8491-5
US $29.95/CAN $35.99

Stay in the Lead and in the Know. Connect with Us

www.pfeiffer.com | www.theleadershipchallenge.com

Follow us on @TLCTalk
Join The Leadership Challenge **Linked** in Group
Become a Fan on

Leadership Is Everyone's Business

Enhance your workshops with Leadership Challenge tools.

Backed by over twenty years of original research, *The Leadership Challenge® Workshop* is an intense discovery process created by bestselling authors, Jim Kouzes and Barry Posner. The workshop demystifies the concept of leadership and leadership development and approaches it as a measurable, learnable, and teachable set of behaviors, establishing a unique underlying philosophy—leadership is everyone's business.

The Leadership Challenge Workshop Facilitator's Guide Set, Fourth Edition
978-0-470-59217-5 | $799.00 US

The all-new *Leadership Challenge Workshop Facilitator's Guide Set, Fourth Edition* includes detailed instructions, suggested experiential activities, audio/video clips including new video case studies, and a facilitator script for a complete training progam. While the ample instructions make for a turnkey solution, the program also allows for and encourages customization points that enable facilitators to tailor the program for their particular audience or situation.

Leadership Practices Inventory (LPI) Action Cards Facilitator's Guide Set
978-0-470-46239-3 | $50.00 US

The Leadership Challenge Activities Book
978-0-470-47713-7 | $50.00 US

The Leadership Challenge Values Cards Facilitator's Guide Set
978-0-470-58007-3 | $50.00 US

A Coach's Guide to Developing Exemplary Leaders: Making the Most of the Leadership Challenge and the Leadership Practices Inventory (LPI)
978-0-470-37711-6 | $45.00 US

The Challenge Continues Facilitator's Guide Set
ISBN 978-0-470-46237-9 | $299.00 US

We also have participant materials in the following languages:
- Spanish
- Simplified Chinese
- German
- French
- Portuguese (available Winter 2011)

Follow us on **twitter** @TLCTalk
Join The Leadership Challenge **Linked in**. Group
Become a Fan on **facebook**

Go to **www.leadershipchallenge.com** to learn more about these products, read case studies, and find the latest research, upcoming events and appearances, and LeaderTalk, The Leadership Challenge blog.

www.leadershipchallenge.com

Pfeiffer™
An Imprint of ⊕WILEY
Now you know.

NOTES

NOTES

NOTES

NOTES

NOTES

NOTES